Higher Mind Awakening

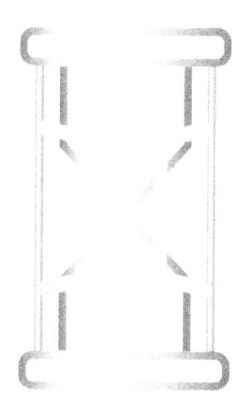

Zaneta Ra

Oracle of the 144

Master of the Pearl Codes

Copyright © 2023 by Zaneta Ra

All Rights Reserved.

No part of this book may be used or reproduced by any means, graphic, electronic, or mechanical, including photocopying, recording, taping, or by any information storage retrieval system without the written permission of the publisher except in the case of brief quotations embodied in critical articles and reviews.

This book is not intended as a substitute for the medical advice of physicians. The reader should regularly consult a physician in matters relating to their health and particularly with respect to any symptoms that may require diagnosis or medical attention.

The information provided in this book is strictly for spiritual educational purposes. If you wish to apply ideas contained in this book, you are taking full responsibility for your actions.

ISBN: 9798397877961

Tarkington Text Press
www.angelicpearls144.com

This book is dedicated to you, the reader. May the wisdom and light encoded in this book ignite, brighten, and expand your light. We will forever fly as one because we are all ONE MIGHTY PEARL.

~*Zaneta Ra*

TABLE OF CONTENTS

TABLE OF CONTENTS 4
INTRODUCTION 7
MIND MAP 11
    Mental Floors 15
    Mind Blueprints 16
THE FEEL WHEEL 23
    Emotional Paint Palette 28
    3D SPECTRUM 30
    5D SPECTRUM 35
    7D SPECTRUM 37
HIGHER MIND ANCHORING 38
    Crowning 39
12 LABOURS OF HERCULES 47
    Stage I 48
    Stage II 58
    Stage III 62
GEMINI 73
    Lower Mind 75

Mind Spectrum 78
   ARCHANGEL METATRON SPEAKS: 79
Mind Prism Exercise 82

ATLANTIS 86

Atlan Mind 91
   ARCHANGEL METATRON SPEAKS: 93

MIND CRYSTALS 97

Andara Crystals 98
Atlantis Crystals 101
Crystal Portals 102

THE NIGHT 105

Dawn Symptoms 107
   Step I 108
   Step II 110
   Step III 112

MIND CODE MEDITATIONS 116

Excerpt from Instill the Grain: Oracles, Gods and Goddesses 132

Excerpt from The Ascension Symptoms Manual 135

Excerpt from Love Letters from Lemuria 137

BOOKS BY ZANETA RA 139

ILLUSTRATIONS 143

INTRODUCTION

The mind is a tool designed to be used for navigation in the dense materialized planes of existence. Just like any tool, if used too often then one will become dependent on that tool. When a child comes into this world, they mostly play because they are not leaning on that mental tool. Instead, they are allowing their heartbeat to shift and sway them. This is why you can feel such pure vibrations emitted from their energy fields.

The mind is a scepter; this is a tool, a device. It is a physical construction, an addition to the physical body. Just like any tool in your possession, you hold control. Where you weld it is where force will follow. The force is the energy that emits from your mind. You have the option to weld it with negative spectrum vibrations or positive spectrum vibrations. No one and nothing outside of you truly controls this. That is merely an illusion.

An illusion to make you feel inferior when the truth is, you are the hero. This life is your story to create, your own journey. Each step you make creates a new footprint in the sand of time. A footprint that no other can make but you. Sometimes those footprints vibrate out to touch others. Sometimes they form a solo path. However, that path is always your own.

Higher Mind Awakening helps you gain better clarity on what the Lower Mind is, its key in Ascension and anchoring the Higher Mind. We break down the sacred coded teachings of becoming the hero through the 12 Labours of Hercules. Hercules is not just one essence; he merely represents the hero expression that is found within you all.

All around you are energetic waves. These waves carry patterns, blueprints that determine a mindset. A mindset that you have the power to choose from. The surfer chooses the wave, the wave does not choose the surfer. It is the surfer who determines if he wants to become one with that wave or allow it to pass him by. To ride the wave, he needs his board. This board is your Higher Mind, and its stability determines your ride.

Who you are in your pureness is not physical at all. You are pure magic that emits from the Mighty Void of No-Thing. You are the golden honey created within the Mighty Beehive of Creation. That very beehive that was born from THE VOID. It is in the darkness that stories are written. Take control of your mind scepter and weave the story you want to be told.

Zaneta Ra: This book is designed as a lesson from the Pearl Code Teachings. It is a simple teaching from the 144 Seraphim on the stage of the **Higher Mind Awakening***. Just like all Pearl Channelings, this book is not edited, to allow the original energy of the Seraphim to flow from the pages to you. The spoken words in the teachings are coded to allow the unspoken codes to ignite within self. You all have the ability to access Divine Wisdom. It starts with conquering the mind.*

"What feeds the mortal mind, does not feed the Spirit. What feeds the Spirit, does not feed the mortal mind."

~*Zaneta Ra*

MIND MAP

As of June 2023, Higher Mind Anchoring activations started for Phase II and III Lightworkers. Phase II are those who mainly awakened in the year 2000 and 2015 for most Grid Workers. Phase III Lightworkers mostly already experienced their Higher Mind Awakening. These are the Souls who awakened in the years of 1972-1993. The main symptom occurring now is the new mind spectrum anchoring *(see **Mind Spectrum** Section).* As you traverse more of your mind map, more spectrums will anchor for you.

This stage of the Ascension journey is for those who already mastered the knowingness of the Ego Mind. Some have already conquered it, while some are in the beginning stages. As you learn about the Higher Mind Anchoring steps, it will help you determine where you are on this journey, where you are on the mind map.

The mind is like a map, where the only compass one can use to navigate it with is an invisible mind crystal. However, to gain access to this crystal, one must balance both the Emotional and Mental Bodies. These bodies are located within the Auric field of a human body and are known as part of the Energy Bodies.

While walking the Ascension pathway you will cross many bridges. At each bridge more of your Christos light will start to illuminate these Energy Bodies. It is at that moment the "dust" held within them will surface. In *Cracking the Chrysalis,* we taught:

> *When you first send out that signal to your Higher Self that you are ready to know who you are, light starts to drip into your crown. This highlights all stuck emotions held within you. Just as you see the dust floating when you let light into your house, so does this process. It shines*

a light so your Higher Self can see all the dust floating in your house. The clean-up process then ignites so all those emotions rise to the surface for healing.

Next to the Emotional Body is the Mental Body. The way you feel is created by your Mental Body because it is fed by your Emotional Body. This is where the saying "mind over matter" comes into play. The matter represents your Physical Body where the mind references your Mental Body.

Think of your Emotional Body like a paint palette in your hand. Each paint color is a different vibrational frequency representing your emotions. The paint brush represents your Mental Body. These tools work together to paint your reality upon the canvas. Each hue of color on the canvas is a match to the mixture you selected. In other words, the vibrations you emit are what help to paint your reality.

During the first stage of awakening, you are learning how to navigate the Emotional and Mental Bodies. It is through the Law of Action that you learn how to balance them and achieve abundance. It takes strong dedication to hold constant self-awareness of your patterns and behaviors while on your awakening journey. Everyone is born into a program of assigned levels of beliefs and structures. This is what molds the ego personality.

~Cracking the Chrysalis:
Shattering the Steps of Ascension

The Law of Action is how you react to the dust that is shown to you. This is accompanied by the program you incarnated into. This program is part of a Mind Blueprint. This is what can determine how you navigate those dust particles that appear along your pathway. Each dust particle is separated by frequency and housed in its own vibrational room. As you reach a new vibrational spectrum, it can be seen as climbing steps to the next floor.

Mental Floors

When it comes to the Mental Body, look at it like a tall multi-floored apartment building. Each floor may appear to look the same, yet when you open each door, they are designed differently. Each room houses different colors, scents, sounds, and energetic imprints. One of the things humans explore in a lifetime is what is behind each door. The key to mastery is to not get stuck too long in each room but continue to explore and move up the levels. When you look at some apartment buildings, most have larger, more luxury condos at the top levels. This goes the same from the Ego layers of the mind. As you ascend the floors, you get closer to wider views.

These wider views are your expanded perception of existence. Each time you raise your vibrational field up an octave, you not only see more, but you also feel more. You can feel more from the lower floors if you simply flow from one to the other. It is when you stay in one room for a long period of time that it develops into an anchor.

The rooms are like emotions. When you suppress them, it is like spending long periods of time in that room. When you allow them to flow, it is like smoothly exploring each room and apartment floor. Suppressed emotions develop into anchors that weigh you down. This highly affects your mind.

"Emotions are the anchors for your mindset. The denser the emotions, the increase of lower vibrational thoughts in your mental field."

~Zaneta Ra

Mind Blueprints

When it comes to a blueprint, you have both an inorganic design and a divine design. The inorganic design holds the key-codes created and imputed by hackers. Where the divine design is one that holds the organic original key-codes created by God Source. The organic grid system is a blue-white diamond plasma spherical sheath, known today as the Sword of Truth or Divine

Will. The Divine Will is a spoken testament by God Source because *The Word* is what physical earthly worlds were created upon. *The Word* is likened to a Divine Command.

When a person is fully connected to their Oversoul/Monad/Pearl-essence, then they are plugged into the organic grid system. They become solely fed via their pillar of light. This pillar can be seen as a giant white Sun beaming into a pearlescent plasma tunnel upon their crown. This light then emits into the great pyramid known as the thalamus.

Just like with any great pyramid, you also have a capstone. The capstone can be seen as the pineal gland. A capstone is an energy conductor designed to send Source energy into a pyramid for it to then Source a grid. The thalamus sends signals of light into the grid system known as the vertebrae of the spine. This is where DNA can then be activated by that same light stream. It then moves to the famous T-cells held in the thymus to finish its full activation. This is where calcium and the pineal gland go together.

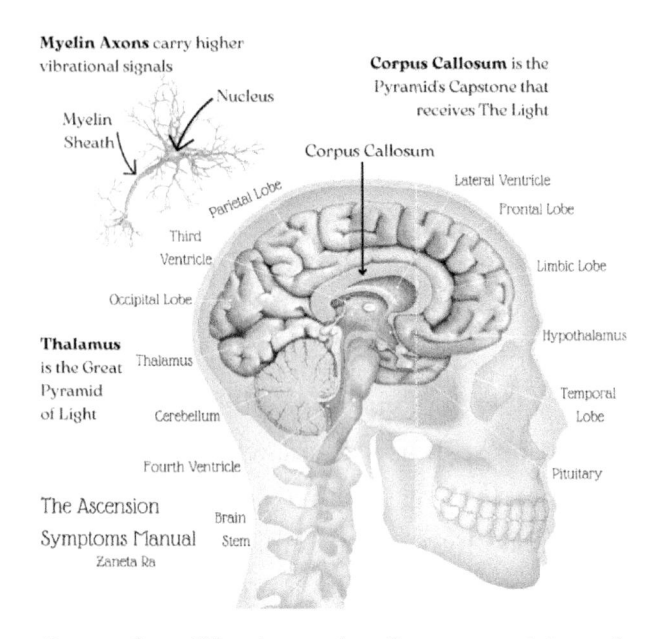

Image from The Ascension Symptoms Manual

Calcium is an energy conductor and key to the pineal gland for igniting these transmissions. The transmission starts with the igniting of the mind capstone, which ignites the depolarization process. Depolarization happens when a cell undergoes a shift in electric charge distribution. This process is key in order for cells to function and communicate with each other. It is during this moment that Voltage-gated calcium channels *(VGCCs)* become activated *(open)*, like a tunnel ready for cars to transport through. An influx of calcium ions is then able to flow into a cell which results in production of gene expression, release of neurotransmitters and hormones, muscle contraction, activation of potassium channels, and more.

When you think of calcium in the pineal gland, think of how wax hardens when it is cooled. When heat *(Christos Light)* is added to the wax, it then melts. This newly heated fluid can now flow like honey into your body. It is the flow of your own Christos Light that naturally allows this process to occur.

When depolarization occurs, it increases the production of cytosol, also known as cytoplasmic matrix. Cytoplasm is where we find mitochondria. When you think of a matrix, you know it is a plasma spherical grid system programmed with keycodes. These codes feed into the living energy fields that reside within it. An example is the matrix of Earth and the codes found within it. These codes are programed and fed as a loop into the DNA of all energy fields that live upon her. Another example is the womb of a mother. The fluid held there is a plasma grid system as well. Hence the teaching in our book

Love Letters from Lemuria, where we spoke of the plasma sheath that surrounds a Universal System. The cells within your human form are the micro expression of a Universe.

With that said, if this natural process, just like any other process seen in nature, is forced, then it will disrupt the natural flow of energy and ultimately the creation itself. When you try to force any of the steps upon the Spiritual Awakening path, it can cause an overload to your nervous systems. This energy then ripples out and causes a disruption in the Universal System as well.

When it comes to the inorganic system, if one is plugged into that, then they are programmed by that design. Meaning that whatever is placed upon that system will flow into the DNA of that living being. This is where trends come into play. Think, why is it that where a person lives determines the language they speak or the way they speak it. Or why is it that clothing attire is one land differs from another land. This is because those people are plugged into a specific grid system.

When it comes to what is so-called trending, those who follow those trends are plugged into that grid system. The system we speak of is the collective human consciousness. This is a grid system that all humans can plug into. Some choose to stay connected into that system. This is their energetic stream where they receive their codes. You have others who choose to plug into their pillar of light.

This is where that more pronounced divide is being seen today. Those who do not fully understand the trends of the masses are because they are plugged solely into their Monad, their Pearl-essence, their Wholeness. Make no mistake, there is no right or wrong here because everything at the end of the day is divine. It also does not mean one is better than the other. It is simply a choice, and we are merely explaining the depths of this topic to you all.

If someone is tapped into the inorganic system, then they are also pulling information from the Astral field. The Astral field is an inorganic plane that houses all the mental energies of the living beings on Earth. All thoughts, beliefs systems, teachings, and so forth of humans reside there. They reside there because this plane is fed by the collective human consciousness field. One must be able to filter through that massive hall of mirrors and illusions to access the true higher planes of existence.

When a consciousness field unplugs from a material form *(body, aka death)*, all the energies held within their Mental Body at that time will then transfer into the Astral. When that same consciousness field reincarnates, it will pull in those same energetic waves as a magnet. This is how one can carry over illusions of so-called past life trauma. This is one of the many reasons why we teach how important it is to fully feel and heal while on your Spiritual Journey.

Gaining a deeper understanding of feelings is key to helping transmute those energy dust balls. This will then give you more mental clarity to use for discerning those consciousness fields. To discern if the energetic waves you feel are yours or the collective.

THE FEEL WHEEL

The mindset you have is based off the six core feelings located in the Emotional Paint Palettes. We designed these palettes to help you dive deep within your Emotional Body and gain better clarity of what is hidden there. Each of these core feelings are a spectrum of light *(wave)* within the vibrational elixir of creation.

Emotions are broken down in a 3rd, 5th, and 7th Density vibrational spectrum. The field that flows into your mind is what determines your emotional playing field. The scale starts with the spectrum of Sadness, Fear, and Anger. These are all part of the 3D spectrum. Next, you have Strength and Happiness. These two are found within the 5D spectrum. Lastly, you have Tranquility, which is the stage of a Light Master.

Higher Mind Awakening
Zaneta Ra

STRENGTH

ANGER　　　　　　HAPPINESS

FEAR　　　　　　TRANQUILITY

SADNESS

The key is to not only achieve your desired spectrum but to maintain balance *(like the surfer)* within that vibrational spectrum. Meaning, that in every now moment your Emotional Body is aligned to that frequency. The longer you vibrate in a spectrum, the more that light wave spectrum can be absorbed into your bones.

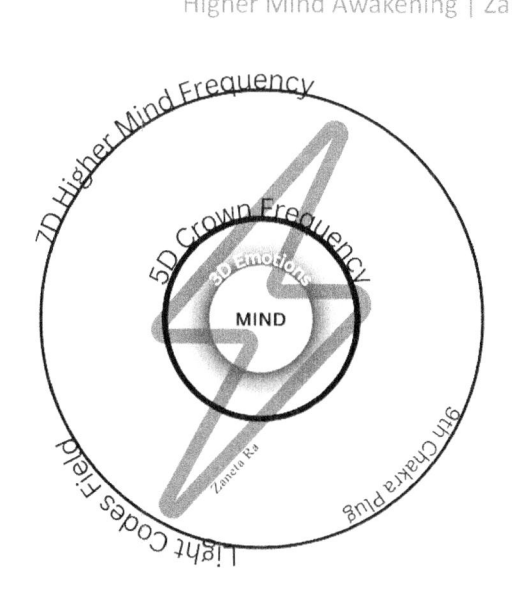

Your bones can be seen as your very own internal crystalline cave. This is where your DNA upgrades start. They start with the electrical currents flowing into your Physical Body via the other Energetic Bodies. Since the Emotional and Mental Bodies are the closest to the Physical Body, if there are any blockages held there then the currents will meet resistance.

Piezoelectric basically is an electric charge that arises in solids like bones, DNA, and crystals (your bones already have tiny crystals in them). Blood cells are produced in bone marrow; therefore, plasma light flows from your Light Codes to then be stored in your bones. Think of your bones as batteries that are charged by your Light Codes (when this is happening it also causes joint pain). These batteries can now be used to "turn on" devices such as blood cells.

~The Ascension Symptoms Manual

These currents flow into you via your Energy Centers *(Chakras)*. These can be seen as vents in your house. If the vents are clogged due to "dust balls" then the flow of energy meets resistance. This can cause more blockages to happen in your other Energy Bodies, such as your Light Body. Balancing those emotions is very important to fully awakening your Kundalini so you can become plugged into your Higher Mind.

Ancient Pearl Code teachings taught of the serpent being coiled and in hibernation at your Sacral Chakra *(below the belly button)*. All of you have a diamond light cord that connects to your belly button and flows directly to Divine Creator. This feeds you that lifeforce energy, as it does to all of creation. Once this area holds no blockages in the Energy Bodies then it will awaken the serpent. With active breathwork, the lifeforce energy is fed into the diamond serpent. This starts the sheading of its skin.

The skin is made of diamond dust which then ignites into the base of your spine. The golden light that is fed via your 9th Chakra *(golden pearl at the base of your skull)* will then drip into your spine to meet this diamond dust. When they touch, they ignite the Kundalini Awakening. The serpent fully transforms to then glide up your spine and eat from the golden apple, better known today as the Golden Chalice *(Medulla Oblongata)*. It is not until the serpent awakens does the Chalice start to fill up. This is why serpents are seen guarding the apple tree and the caduceus in ancient teachings.

Zaneta Ra: *The serpent advising Eve to eat the apple is decoded here. The tree is your Soul Tree that your light seeded to Earth from. The Garden, well that is an unseen layered destination.*

The Golden Chalice
The Ascension Symptoms Manual
Zaneta Ra

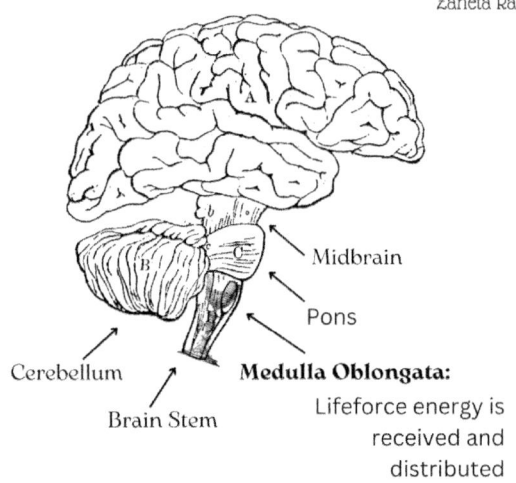

- Midbrain
- Pons
- **Medulla Oblongata:** Lifeforce energy is received and distributed
- Cerebellum
- Brain Stem

Emotional Paint Palette

It is at the Tranquility Spectrum that a true Kundalini Awakening is ignited. One may have felt the serpent start to uncoil, but the full awakening feels like hot lava being poured down your spine. Your back will arch up, some may experience small convulsions. Lastly, it will feel as if peppermint is running through your veins 24/7. The peppermint feeling is the pure Christos Light flowing from your Light Body. Most will get small doses of this feeling to adjust the form prior to the awakening.

This starts the stage of Enlightenment along your journey. Each of the six core feelings is associated with a specific Energy Center.

SADNESS: ROOT CHAKRA
FEAR: SACRAL CHAKRA
ANGER: SOLAR PLEXUS
STRENGTH: HEART CHAKRA
HAPPINESS: CROWN CHAKRA
TRANQUILITY: 9TH CHAKRA

The first stage is to collapse all suppressed emotions of the 3D spectrum. This will start to slowly collapse the lower three Chakras to allow your new anchor point to be in your Heart Chakra. This is where the Christ Seed *(see **Cracking the Chrysalis:** Shattering the Steps of Ascension for the teaching)* can be anchored, the blooming of the Blue Pearl, your Higher Heart.

Those of you who have stomach issues are due to a blockage at your Solar Plexus. This is associated with the Anger Stage and connected directly to your gut. Anger is simply depression mirrored inward.

The Strength stage is at the higher 4D and lower 5D spectrums, where Happiness is within the 5D spectrum. The Happiness stage is the start of expansion for your consciousness. This is directly connected to your Crown Chakra.

3D SPECTRUM

How to work with each Emotional Paint Palette:

Each Emotional Paint Palette houses 6 internal emotions surrounded by 6 external emotions. Each Palette houses the vibrational frequency number of its spectrum.

When you have a feeling, go to the Palettes to find it. Look at both the internal and external emotions and go within to identify the anchor of them. Allow the energy associated with this vibration to surface and flow. Then follow these 5 steps:

1-Remove the emotional label to view it simply as energy.

2-Remove any identity you have attached to it.

3-Remove from your energy field to allow your consciousness to refocus.

4-Remove any mental power and energy you projected towards this energy.

5-Remove any cords with this energy and ask your spirit team to take over. Conclude with 3 slow deep breaths.

Higher Mind Ascending
SADNESS <100

Zaneta Ra

- Inferior
- Unmotivated
- Depressed
- Isolated
- Fragile
- Lonely
- Hurt
- Neglected
- Regretful
- Betrayed
- Rejected
- Hopeless

©Zaneta Ra 2023

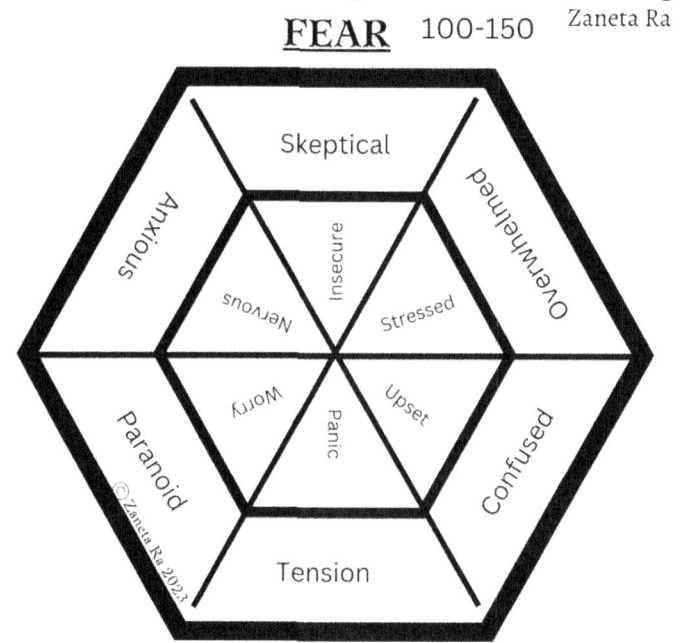

Higher Mind Ascending
FEAR 100-150
Zaneta Ra

- Skeptical
- Anxious
- Overwhelmed
- Insecure
- Nervous
- Stressed
- Worry
- Panic
- Upset
- Paranoid
- Confused
- Tension

© Zaneta Ra 2023

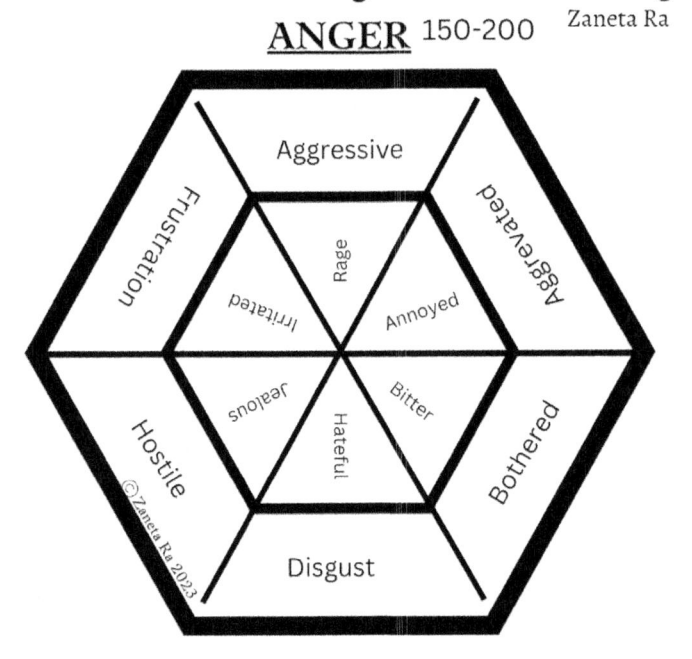

Higher Mind Ascending
ANGER 150-200 — Zaneta Ra

- Aggressive
- Aggrevated
- Bothered
- Disgust
- Hostile
- Frustration

Inner ring: Rage, Annoyed, Bitter, Hateful, Jealous, Irritated

5D SPECTRUM

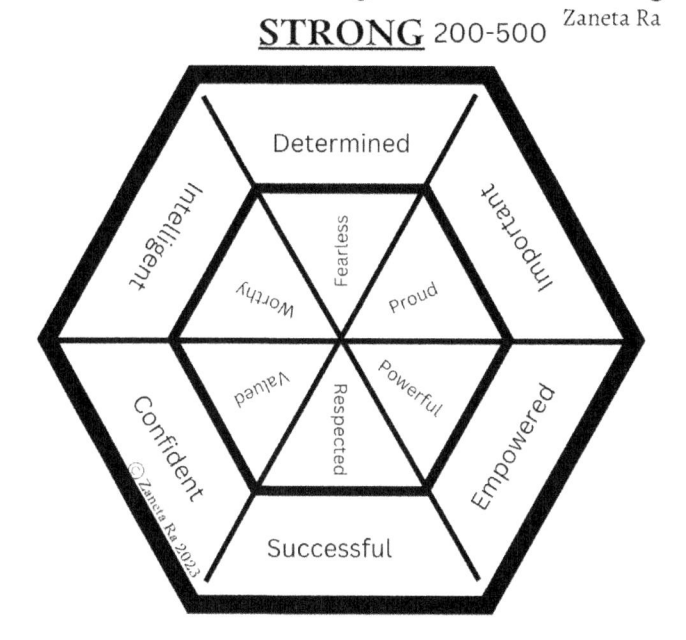

Higher Mind Ascending
STRONG 200-500 Zaneta Ra

- Determined
- Intelligent
- Important
- Fearless
- Worthy
- Proud
- Valued
- Powerful
- Confident
- Respected
- Empowered
- Successful

© Zaneta Ra 2023

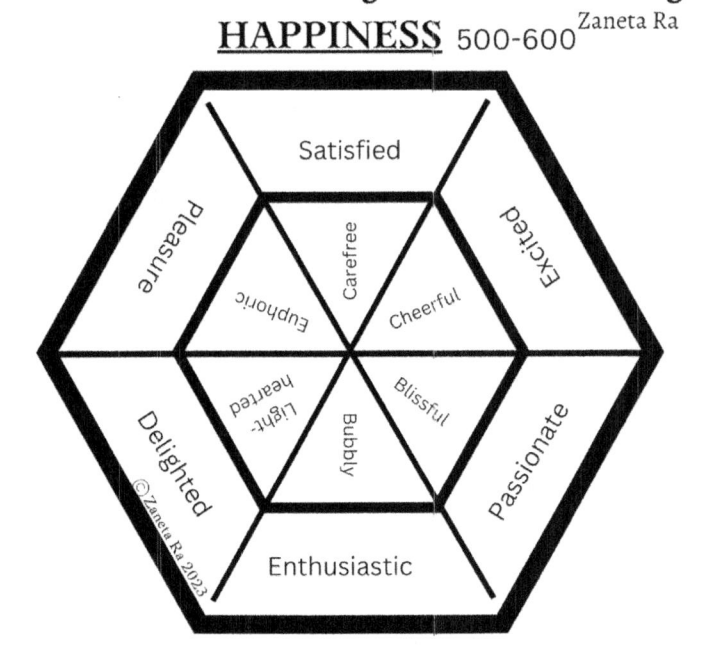

Higher Mind Ascending
HAPPINESS 500-600

- Satisfied
- Pleasure
- Excited
- Carefree
- Euphoric
- Cheerful
- Light-hearted
- Bubbly
- Blissful
- Delighted
- Passionate
- Enthusiastic

© Zaneta Ra 2023

7D SPECTRUM

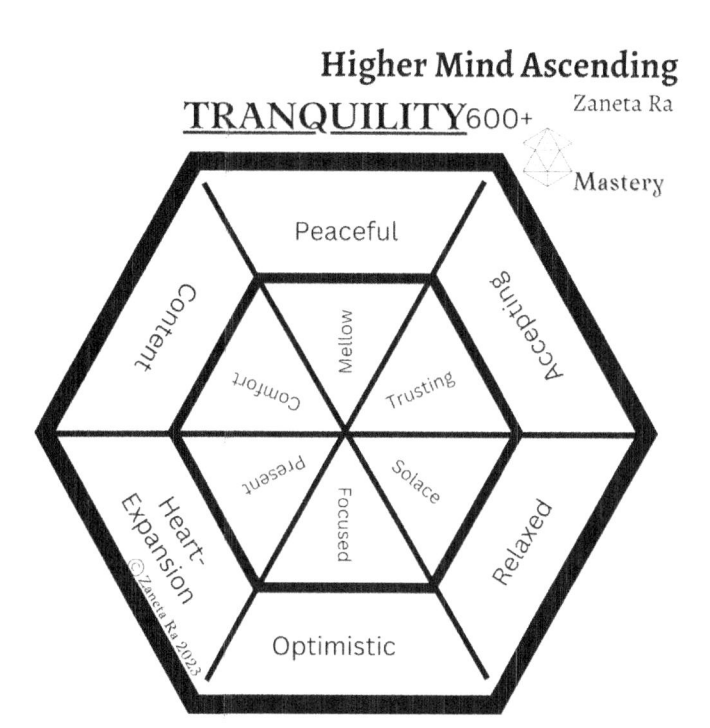

Higher Mind Ascending

TRANQUILITY 600+ — Zaneta Ra

Mastery

- Peaceful
- Content
- Accepting
- Heart-Expansion
- Relaxed
- Optimistic
- Mellow
- Comfort
- Trusting
- Present
- Focused
- Solace

©Zaneta Ra 2023

HIGHER MIND ANCHORING

The flow of emotions are the vibrations of the water particles from the river of life. Particles that fall like rain into the realms of Earth. They help to water, nourish, and expand the seeds. Seeds are born in the darkness, are they not. This water helps them to expand and grow out of that darkness, out of the depths and to expand above ground. However, they also expand further into the ground as well.

With each emotion you dance with, it helps you to expand your roots deeper. These roots help you to feel more, while the stem helps you to receive more light and wisdom. The stem is your pillar of light. As the stem ascends, it expands to allow this light to anchor. This is the Higher Mind Anchoring occurring.

If a seed is still forming in the ground, how can it receive the gold dust *(pollen)*. It is through *feelings* that help you to become grounded enough for this expansion to occur. The more expanded your roots, the more you will feel. This is where you are now. This is why you long for serenity. It is because you are more sensitive to the vibrations of the river of life.

These vibrations help to mold your Light Body. You are a diamond in the making. Emotions are the pressure needed for this transformation. The key here is to simply feel them, acknowledge them as vibrations from the river of life. As you shift this perception it will allow them to flow through you, which will then allow your expansion to flow more smoothly. This will allow the Ego to quiet and succumb to the flow of the river. To then merge as one with the wave.

Crowning

When your Crown Chakra has expanded to allow the anchoring to occur, it can be seen as keeping your head above ground. In the previous image, you see the head is placed above the ground. There is a starlight above it. This light is the anchor seed to allow light signals from your Higher Mind in.

As these signals rain down, they start to form a diamond egg around you. This starts to fill up with wisdom/codes from your Higher Mind. Your pillar of light is like a radio tower. The signals it is now receiving come from your Higher Mind. This is the communication device between your incarnate essence and your Pearl-essence/Monad/Oversoul.

A radio station can lose signal if the car travels outside of its perimeter. Your Lower Mind is driving your physical vehicle at this stage. In those states where your mind is wondering, it can be seen as traveling. In those overactive mind moments, this can be seen as driving the car too fast. In both cases it will cause your radio station to lose signal. When you stay centered, it keeps your mind within the perimeter to receive signals clearly.

In the Higher Mind Anchoring image, you also see a flashlight effect at the top. This is your Higher Mind emitting light into your pillar of light. This is meant to help show you "The Way". When you connect to this light, it will shine onto the path for you. This is the pathway to receiving your Cap/Crowning.

Once the diamond light egg has encased you completely, this light will always emit from you. What this means is that if you turn from the path where you are focusing, this light will emit towards that direction. A prime example we are seeing right now are those who are distracted by assisting others on their path. What is occurring unconsciously is that the person is reaching out to your light. This light is now taken off your path and instead shining their way to help them see more clearly. This is when you have those steps where you feel pulled away from your journey.

Where you feel unmotivated and unable to fully focus.

Once you turn back towards your own path, then you will become realigned with your center. The grand saying with the final stage of Ascension is that you are to walk it alone. That final pathway is always done in solitude. It is done this way to remove those distractions. Some are masters at handling them while others are not.

Before graduation, one will receive their cap and gown. In Ascension the Cap is the Crowing of your Higher Mind. While the Gown is the rainbow robe.

> *"Behold the Lamb of God who takes away the sin of the world." John 1:29 KJV*

Sin was taken from the Hebrew word hata which originated from the Norse hata meaning *to hate*. The original meaning of hate was *to block* or *shield*. This is where the word hat stems from. What this means in the original teachings is that only when your Crown Chakra fully opens can your Christos light come in. This is the process of removing your mortal hat/cap to allow the

Higher Mind to anchor. This is when you receive your Cap for graduation.

When you receive the Cap, see it as a flashlight shining above your head. This light is reflected off the plasma sheath walls of the diamond egg around you. It is during this process that you will physically see diamond sparkles of light *(some call them orbs)* around you *(especially in the Sunlight)*. During meditation you will see them in your mind's eye as well. We listed this symptom under the *Physical Symptoms: Senses* section of ***The Ascension Symptoms Manual***:

> • ***Seeing Diamond Sparkles:*** *When salt is in a fire it alters the electrons and causes the salt to release photons of light. When looking at this it appears as golden sparks. These photons of light are what we are transforming into. These photons of light are all around us. Therefore, as the Solar Flares blast and reach our Lower Atmosphere it changes the electrons in the air causing us to see flashes of tiny diamond lights. The Earth and all*

living beings upon her are slowly entering the Sun. As we get closer, more heat is added causing these magical phenomena.

~The Ascension Symptoms Manual

What is occurring is the space between those diamond light photons are decreasing. As they decrease it will cause them to unite and spark. Salt is multi-dimensional, and this is in your Higher DNA now anchoring around you. Once the unification process is complete, they form your Rainbow Robe/Rainbow Body/Diamond Body. This is the pearlescent plasma light that transforms you. This is when you have conquered THE NIGHT.

Higher Mind Awakening
Zaneta Ra

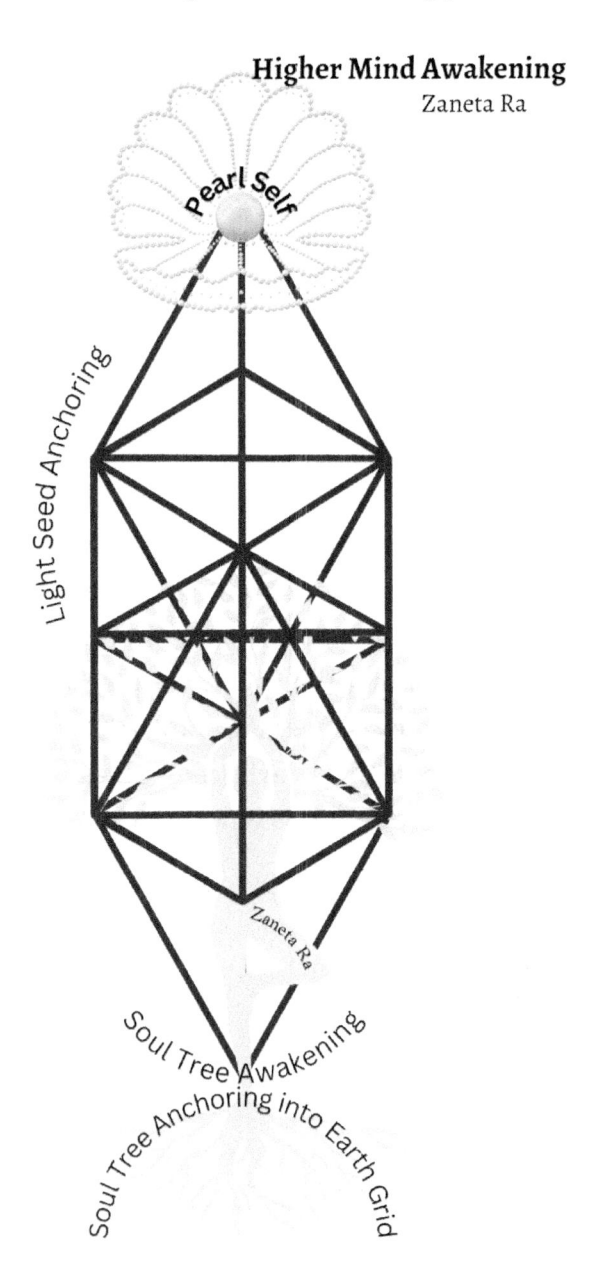

Pearl Self

Light Seed Anchoring

Zaneta Ra

Soul Tree Awakening

Soul Tree Anchoring into Earth Grid

12 LABOURS OF HERCULES

Before the time of physical record keeping, lessons were taught by way of stories. We teach in *Angelic Pearls 144* how the Solar Tribes came to this plane to anchor the Flame of Love. Love is The Way to Spiritual Enlightenment because it is existence itself. Throughout existence you have those who worship the Flame of Love and those who worship the Flame of Power. As the spectrums of Love and Power became unbalanced, the coded layers of the teachings became lost.

The story of the 12 Labours of Hercules is a coded teaching of the 12 Steps to conquering the night.

The 12 Steps one must conquer before Ascending the Underworld. One of the guardians of the doorway that leads from the Underworld to the God Worlds is Hercules. Hercules is a vibrational aspect that translates to "Glory of Hera". You learn in *Instill the Grain: Oracles, Gods and Goddesses* that Hera is the expression of Time/Mortal Existence. Therefore, the 12 Labours of Hercules is about becoming the victor of the mortal body, which is Physical Ascension.

We will break down each of the coded Ascension Stairsteps held within this sacred teaching from the times of antiquity. The 12 Labours are divided into three stages, with three steps in each. This teaching is the handbook of the *Higher Mind Awakening*.

Stage I

Step 1: *Slay the Nemean Lion.*

This step is about conquering the roar of the mind, that mind chatter. In mythology the Ladon Serpent is seen as the brother of the Nemean Lion and a guard of the golden apples. We taught earlier how the golden apples are the fruit from your golden chalice. The fruit that is accessed from your own Tree of Life.

Caduceus

The spine can also be seen as the trunk of a tree. The roots are grounded into the soil, Earth, where the branches expand upward into the God Worlds, Air. This is where the legends of the World Tree stem from. The World spoken of in the ancient temples was about the entire Mortal World. We called this the Axis Mundi which is known today as the naval of the world.

~Instill the Grain: *Oracles, Gods and Goddesses*

It is not until one quiets the roar of the lion can one hear the whispers of their Spirit. Each roar is linked to those suppressed emotions we previously spoke of.

Picture dust clogging your air vent in your home. Now visualize air trying to flow through that vent with maximum force. You will see how small dust particles are falling from the clogged dust. Another example is when a vent in a dryer has not been emptied. When you finally go to empty it, you see multiple dust particles flying in the air around you. These particles are small energy droplets from those suppressed emotions that flow into your mind as "chatter".

What is occurring is the mind is selecting a labeled expression that has a like vibration to that energy droplet. The mind is programmed at birth via ancestral DNA to label the energy it feels. It is then conditioned by all the verbal expressions it records during interactions and observations of the incarnate. Meaning that if someone is observing an emotional expression for the first time and overhears someone label it with a feeling, then the Mental Body stores that as an identity. Energy simply "is". When you label it, you divide it. This type of division by default causes your consciousness to divide and eventually become fractalized.

This is where reprogramming identities and labels of emotions is important to collapsing the ego personalities. Which leads us to the second labour.

Step 2: *Slay the nine-headed Lernaean Hydra.*

This step is about collapsing the nine Ego layers of the mind. Lernaean in Mythology resides at the entrance of the Underworld. This is the portal that allows one to traverse the 3D planes of reality and enter the Unseen Worlds. It is only when you conquer Lernaean do you ascend from the depths of your mind. These depths are likened to the depths of the Ocean or the Underworld.

Hercules by John Singer Sargent 1921

The Ego Mind is a programmed mainframe designed to assist in navigating 3D planes. The organic mind is the Higher Mind which was created at the time your Soul Elixir was designed by God Source. The Ego Mind is inorganic and is an artificial intelligence controlled by a negative motherboard that keeps one from seeing past the veils. This is designed to keep humans from operating from their heart and instead to operate from their emotions. Hence the wise saying: *"Do not let your emotions get the best of you."*

In order to operate with a clear mind, the energies of the Emotional Body must be balanced first. Remember, the paint palette you choose from is determined by your Emotional Body. This is what you use to paint upon your reality canvas. Where you focus your mind *(thoughts)* is where energy will be projected. This energy is what determines what is manifested in your reality. If you project out lower vibrations such as negative thoughts, then this will manifest in your field. If you project out higher vibrations such as positive thoughts, then this will manifest in your field. This is the Laws of Action because it is your action that causes a like attraction to manifest around you.

Step 3: *Capture the Ceryneian Hind.*

This speaks about the white stag. We taught in **Instill the Grain:** *Oracles, Gods and Goddesses* that the white stag protects the Christos energy. This is symbolized by Sagittarius upon the Zodi Act wheel.

> *We needed to create serpent barriers **(Ophiuchus)** that bring life, the pure Christos to these bodies. We then needed to protect this energy and who gains access to this, so it does not overload the dense bodies, so we created Archers/Guardians **(Sagittarius).** This essence holds guard over the serpent breath, the Divine Wisdom.*
>
> *~**Instill the Grain:** Oracles, Gods and Goddesses*

The stag is directly connected to the goddess Artemis because she is one of the guardians of the Christos energy. The Christos is depicted to be fed from a sacred garden. This is why deer and other animals are seen in mythology with guardians like Artemis. Once you have collapsed the nine Ego layers, then you are able to expand your consciousness to allow the Christos energy to drip into your field.

In the original story of this labour it speaks of Hercules capturing the stag with a net. This net is the golden net of the Christos vibrations that emit from your mind. This is what starts to create the honeycombs for your spiritual beehive also known as your Light Body.

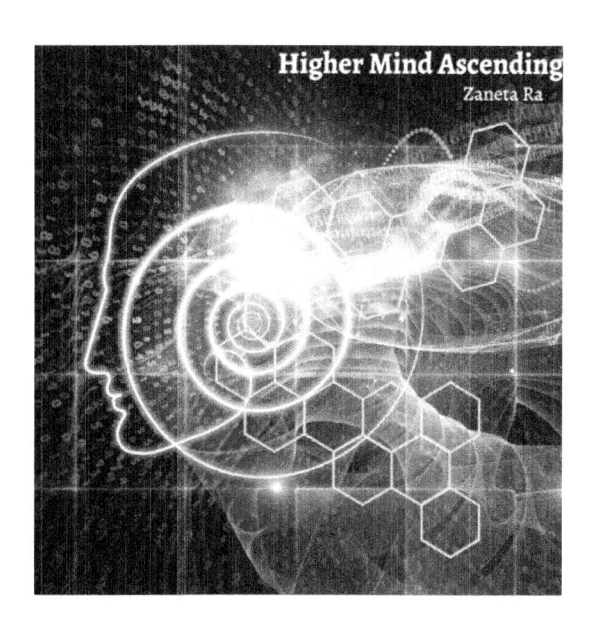

As these honeycombs start to anchor around you, they are then able to produce honey. This honey is the sacred nectar of your Pearl-essence/Monad. In the Higher Dimensions honey is seen as fairy dust. We teach this as *Golden Dust* in **Angelic Pearls 144**. This golden dust can be seen as plasma honey in the Lower Dimensions.

Held within this are Light Codes. As the toroidal field around your mind rises in frequency, you will gain access to these Light Codes. See the Light Codes as a locked book of knowledge. The key to open the book is a specific hertz frequency. When you stabilize your mind to this hertz frequency, then the book will be pulled into your Crown Chakra like a tornado collecting debris. It will then unlock and dissolve as light into your conscious mind. This is why people can gain access to information in certain meditative states.

Bee-goddess, perhaps associated with Artemis above female heads. Gold plaques, 7th century BC

Seen in the Bee-goddess image are 8-petaled rosettes. These are associated with the opening of the 8th Chakra, which is the Higher Heart. This is when you start to shift from operating from a 4-

chamber physical heart to an 8-petal crystalline one. The wings denote expansion of the consciousness. When you reach this stage of expansion, it can be seen as wings emitting from your mind. It resembles wings because it is tiny hair thin rays of light emitting from your mind, which cause the illusion of wings in the Lower Density planes.

Step 4: *Capture the Erymanthian Boar.*

Bears eat from a field, that sacred garden that houses the Christos, the HONEY. Bears in the ancient past were depicted with the goddess Artemis for this reason. The vibration of *Art* is associated with bears and can be seen with other bear deities such as the Celtic *Art*io and And*art*a. Even the word art itself is associated with the Christos energy. When you do artistic activities, it allows your channels to open so the sacred honey can flow into you. This is that creative energy from the depths of your Soul. This is when you are anchored in your heART, anchored in the now moment.

The bear is seen as your thoughts. Your thoughts feed your mind. When you capture them, you become in control of them. It is when you do this that you gain control of your magical mind scepter. This scepter receives the magic honey from your Christos. This is seen as the bear eating honey from the sacred garden. When you master what the bear eats, you become a master of the mind.

Stage II

Step 5: *Clean the Augean Stables in a Day.*

The word Augean means *bright*. The stables symbolize your pillar of light that feeds your Crown Chakra, which houses your mind. Unbalanced thoughts can be seen as wild horses running. It can even feel as if they are running in your mind when that mind chatter is overactive. This in turn causes anxiety.

When the stable for the wild horse is clean, it means that the masculine and feminine energies are balanced. This is that balance between the left and right side of your mind. When this is balanced, it allows the light to flow from your Crown Chakra smoothly.

Step 6: *Slay the Stymphalian Birds.*

The Stymphalian birds in mythology reside in a swamp. They symbolize the Astral thought-forms, those inorganic mind particles. The Astral houses all that emits as a thought from the Emotional and Mental Bodies of the collective. These thoughts are known as Astral Particles.

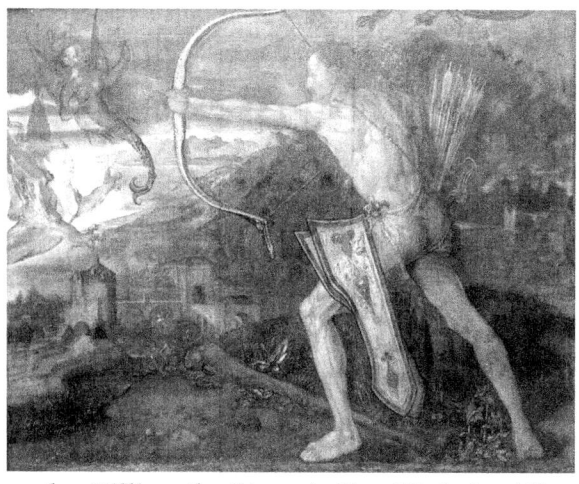

Hercules Killing the Stymphalian Birds by Albrecht Durer, 1500

The Astral particles are from all who have ever incarnated here. They include fragmented portions of the Emotional and Mental Bodies of Souls that became stuck within the Astral Plane at the time of death. This is symbolized by the swamp that the Stymphalian birds reside in. The Astral Plane is a polarity field because it houses both positive and negative particles.

The very thoughts that enter the mind of someone on their awakening path are these particles. It is only when the person chooses to feed energy to a particle does it grow, and if it is fed enough energy then it can become propelled to take on a form. Slaying the Stymphalian birds is slaying these Astral Particles.

Zaneta Ra: *Visualize the energy field around you expanding in size. As it expands, it is encasing all energy waves around it. There will come a time when you encase the entire Astral Body of the collective. This is that step. As your consciousness expands, so does your Light Body. It merges with your Soul Tree in The Garden. You are also part of Earth's Tree and her Seed Crystal (Inner Sun). You must ascend past the Astral waves to receive your full Crowning. The gates of the Astral are where most are currently upon this Timeline. It is because of this stage that you will feel the surges from Earth's Inner Sun, her own Solar Flashes (Energy Waves).*

Step 7: *Capture the Bull.*

We taught in the Zodi Act teachings *(Instill the Grain)* that Taurus represents the mind shell. This originally was seen as a tortoise because its shell holds the body. The body is your Higher Mind, the consciousness spark anchored in your Crown. Later the symbol became the bull.

Capturing the bull is coded for opening your Crown so this light seed can fully connect to you. This is when the sacred wisdom that is held within your Higher Mind can flow into you. This is the start of becoming plugged into the Metatronic Mind, which is the Universal Mind. In ancient Egypt the Apis Bull is seen with the golden Sun Disk. This denotes the Higher Mind anchoring in the mind shell.

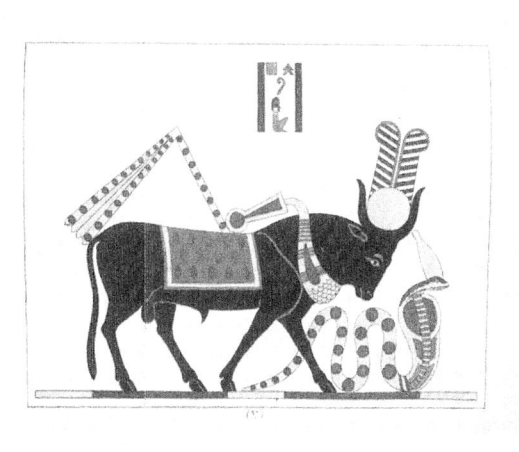

Apis Bull

Another story of a hero capturing a bull is in Meitei folklore. It speaks of the Kao Bull captured by Khuman Khamba. Are not all of you on a hero's journey as well. A journey to capture the bull.

Step 8: *Steal the Mares of Diomedes.*

The Mares of Diomedes represent the masculine and feminine energy of your essence. Step 5 is about balancing those energies, where this step is about anchoring them.

These horses are seen in mythology as "man eating". What this means is that when you anchor them, you are starting the dematerialization process of the flesh. This is the beginning stages of a Physical Ascension.

Stage III

Step 9: *Obtain the girdle of Hippolyta, Amazon Queen.*

The girdle is a belt. It represents the diamond umbilical cord that connects to your belly button. This cord connects to the Cosmic Ocean of Creation. Pure lifeforce energy is fed into your field through this cord. You can also use this cord to remove from your energy field all that no longer serves you. As it enters this cord it is transmuted and balanced into love, then sent to God Source.

This belt is depicted in ancient days with a double spiral that feds into a stream. The spirals are represented by the horns of a ram. These two spirals signify the first thought that emitted from THE MIND of God Source. It is from these spirals that Light Seeds were created. Light Seeds are the elixirs of Souls that were created in the Angelic Realms, we call them Pearls. Balls of light laced in 144 rainbow ribbon rays of Creation.

Higher Mind Ascending
Zaneta Ra

The Girdle of Hippolyta

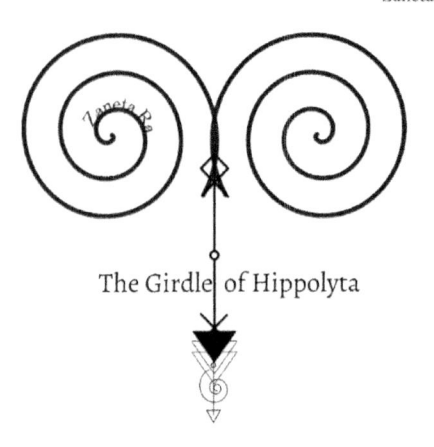

It is these 144 rays of light that are fed in your diamond light cord. This diamond light sparkles with all the rays of Creation. The very rays that you are. This is also depicted in the ancient Pearl Temple teachings via the Isis Knot *(Tyet)*.

Isis knot, Tyet 1550-1275 BC

The Tyet is the famous symbol for the goddess Isis. This is because the loop at the top represents the Divine womb, the start of all of Creation.

From Divine Source the first contraction (thought wave) split into two, represented by the two arms. The horn stem is the sound wave that went out from the Mighty Mind to create all of Creation. Just like the Ishtar Gate, you have here the four marks (under the loop) representing the four templates of Creation. The arms have a line down the center as a representation of balance. The balancing of the light and shadow side that resides in every Soul Spark. The Divine 72 essences of shadow and 72 essences of light emitted from The Womb dance everywhere in existence.

*~**Rising Merits**: The 42 Pearl Temples of Ancient Egypt*

Step 10: *Obtain the cattle of the three-bodied giant Geryon.*

Geryon in mythology is seen as the grandson of Medusa. The snakes of Medusa merely represent thought-forms. All of creation is simply a thought-form from the Mighty Mind of Creator. What this symbolizes is the collection of the Tri-Fold Flame Heart Crystal energy.

Geryon's father is Chrysaor which symbolizes the *gold sword*. Geryon's mother is Callirhoe which symbolizes the *stream*. This is a coded teaching about the birthing of a creation from the spoken word *(gold=**Christos** + sword=**Divine Will**)* that flows into the river of life. That golden dust that flows travels through the plasma river of existence.

Going back to the image of the girdle, notice the upside-down pyramid. This signifies that energy. The energy from the Divine Masculine and Divine Feminine *(Creator)* that seeded your Light. Hence why we call you all Light Seeds. You were seeded from THE LIGHT. This formation creates the sacred triangle shape. The unification of all three Light Pillars, the foundation of your existence *(core of the Mer Ka Ba symbol)*. However, keep in mind this is how it is seen in the lower dimensions.

St. Mark's Basilica, Venice Floor mosaic by Paolo Uccello, Small stellated dodecahedron

The next stage is the creational body of the Light Seed. We teach this as the Vahana in **Angelic Pearls 144**. This is the spiritual body that your elixir uses to travel throughout all of existence.

When your elixir sends out a spark of itself into a Material Plane, then it creates extensions. These are those other 11 aspects of self that will merge with you, creating 12 to then ascend as one into your Higher Self.

When you look upon the Light Seed image, notice how Universal Creations *(Universe=Dimension)* are a dodecahedron. Everything in existence contracts and expands. Notice the Light Seed points when it is expanded. This occurs when the Light Seeds themselves expand. The energy released in that moment causes portals to then open into new realities, densities, and dimensions.

As you anchor your Higher Mind, you are centralized within your Light Seed Crystal. See how the Mer Ka Ba symbol encases the Tri-Fold Flame Crystal, this is that anchor point. All the energy waves streaming into it are Universal Thought Wave Fields *(timelines)*. Where you align your consciousness is the field you will ascend into. First, you begin streaming its energy into your Mental Body. This is why there are many timeline teachings on your plane now. It is up to you which one you want to anchor upon.

Higher Mind Ascending
Light Seed
Zaneta Ra

Masculine Feminine

Light Seed
Emanated

Light Seeded
in Material Planes

© Zaneta Ra 2023

Contracted   Universal
             Creations   Expanded

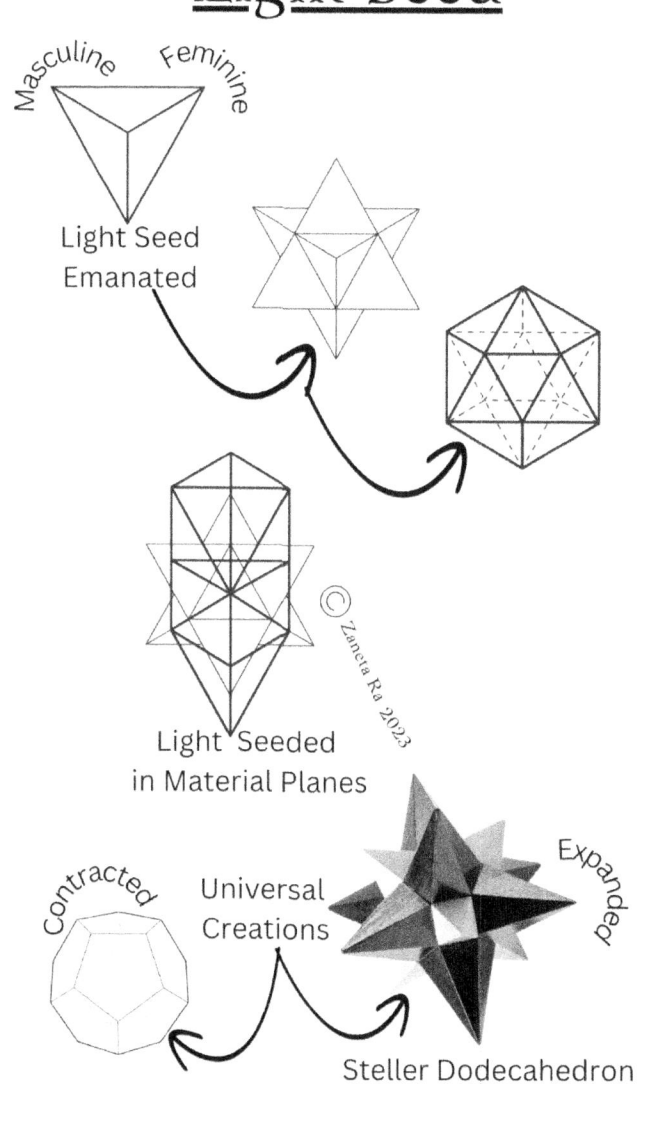

Steller Dodecahedron

Step 11: *Steal the 3 golden apples of Hesperides.*

This is that anchoring of the Light Seed within and without you. This is seen in ancient, coded teachings as the Trident, the Fleur-de-lis, the Lilly, the Christ Seed and many more.

Hesperides symbolizes Venus. As we have taught in the Pearl Codes teachings this simply represents your Higher Self. Retrieving the 3 golden apples from your Higher Self is you retrieving that anchor of your Light Seed. Hence why the anchor and the Trident connect to water. As we stated earlier, water symbolizes the Underworld.

When you reside within the depths of the Ocean there comes a moment when you send that S.O.S. signal to your Higher Self. Once you complete the first 10 steps, the light anchor will descend into the water. The reason the first 10 steps are to be completed first is because you are to ascend some to meet your Higher Self. Your Lower Self can ascend to a certain vibrational octave, just as your Higher Self can without causing harm to your Light Body.

It is when you connect to your Light Seed anchor that a pillar of light will expand to lift you up.

Step 12: *Capture and bring back Cerberus.*

Cerberus is an aspect of the Egyptian god Anubis or the Norse guard dog Garm. The judgement day in the Book of the Dead shows how Anubis escorts the living into the Horus gateway.

> *As one passes the gates of the 4D bridge they are escorted by the god Anubis. The weight of the heart to that of a feather is judged. This is the only true judgement that takes place at the time when the ascension gates open. The heart becomes heavy, how? It is when you hold onto emotions, which causes dis-ease. It will cause a blockage of energy in all layers of your energetic bodies. This is the meaning of baggage and why we teach you to let go of all that keeps you anchored in this realm. Your goal in this lifetime is to cut those cords so you can ascend like a*

*feather when your sun gateway
opens.*

~Rising Merits

Capturing Cerberus is about the final moment when your guardian appears to escort you across the rainbow bridge. This signifies the portal of pearlescent light you transform into, the Rainbow Body.

> *"You pull the tainted into the light for transformation. As it passes through the plasma sheath walls it is cleansed in pure white light. It passes through layers of light spectrums for realignment and balance. It will slowly sit at the center of the light for rehabilitation. It is at that step new blueprints and mind maps will become molded. When the anchoring has completed, the reborn seed will exit. As it passes back through the plasma sheath walls, it becomes coated with new armor. "*

~Archangel Michael

GEMINI

The Gemini symbol *(as seen on the inside cover of this book)* is an ancient symbol for the rainbow bridge. It is pictured inside of an hourglass because that represents the time portal. This is the Horus gateway used to travel between the Earthly Worlds and the God Worlds. In ancient Norse mythology, it also speaks of the rainbow bridge Bilröst that connects Midgard *(Earth)* and Asgard *(God Worlds)*.

One of the guardians of the doorways exiting the Earthly Worlds is Hercules, along with his twin sons. The pillars of Hercules originally teach this portal system. In Mesopotamian mythology, Meslamta-EA is a guardian as well. We teach in **Cracking the Chrysalis** that EA is a title for "Head of the Earthly Worlds". This is simply a guardian of those Earth portals. Meslamta means the *one who has risen from the Underworld* because of his duty as the portal guard.

Higher Mind Ascending
Zaneta Ra

In ancient Egypt the Gemini symbol was associated with the Sphinx. A Sphinx is seen as a human head on a lion body with wings. What this signifies is the merging of your Angelic Human essence with that of the Earth. It represents the moment when your own twin essence becomes one. Your twin essence is your Higher Self and your Lower Self. It has always been within you, not without.

Hidden behind frequency under the physical Egyptian Sphinx are chambers that lead to a Mystery Temple. This is the Temple of Anubis. Many Moons ago, initiates who were at Step 12 of their Higher Mind Ascending would go there. They would seek to meet Anubis and be escorted into hidden realms.

The Sphinx is the combination of elements. The human head represents Earth. The lion's form represents Fire. The wings represent Air. The final merger is with Water. This is when Anubis escorts you across the Cosmic Waters for you to pass through a diamond plasma waterfall to become transformed.

Lower Mind

The Lower Mind is a mainframe designed for the human body to navigate dense reality planes with.

Mainframe In Navigational Density

This mainframe assists with discernment and identification. In the Lower Densities there are a mixture of organic and inorganic fields. This also can be seen as a connection to the Gemini symbol. That reflection of shadows and light. When you are standing between the pillars, they look the same. This is as if walking through the hall of mirrors and illusions.

When any of the lower spectrum vibrations enter your mind, it causes confusion and chaotic thoughts to form. This is when shielding yourself from them multiplying is important. This shielding is accomplished by discernment and focus. Picture one locust swarming around you. It may be tolerable but, if need be, you can shield yourself from it. Now picture 1,000 locusts swarming towards you. This will be a lot harder to shield. The locust symbolizes chaotic thoughts created by inorganic energy fields.

These are designed to distract you. What makes this existence unique is that you are mastering how to be a Light Worker in a place with unlimited distractions. It is so easy to become like Alice and travel further down the rabbit hole. When you do this, it is multiplying the thoughts in the Lower Mind. This is a vibration that will attract those same vibrations into your field. This is what causes people to become addicted to rabbit holes.

This is why the story of Medusa turning men is stone is taught. The snakes represent those locusts' thoughts. They are what keep you stuck on time loops, frozen in time.

"Time is a sphere, and you are encased within it. If you walk forward, the sphere moves with you. If you walk backwards, the sphere moves with you. You control the sphere; the sphere does not control you."

*~Zeus from **Instill the Grain: Oracles, Gods and Goddesses***

See time as the Ocean, with each wave being a timeline. Go with the current and you will always succeed. It is when you fight the waves that you fail. Only the ocean controls the waves. In life you paddle when they come, don't look back and trust the flow of the current. This is how you live in the "now" moment. This is how you anchor your consciousness within your heart because its wholeness exists within the "now".

When you are anchored in your heart, then your very own vibrational elixir is streaming through you. This is then emitting from your field causing you to attract that of the same frequency. This is when those moments happen along your spiritual journey where you feel you found your tribe. What is occurring is the collective consciousness of your own Soul Tree reuniting. As this unification takes place it allows a portal to open. This then causes the vibrational spectrum of the 144 to anchor upon the Earth grid.

Mind Spectrum

You have 144 vibrational spectrums of THE MIND *(God Source)*. Within them are 144,000 hairline light streams carrying unlimited light particles. These 144 spectrums consist of 72 shadow and 72 light frequencies. Now, view the Sadness frequency *(paint palette 1)* as one of light streams. Held within it are unlimited particles. Meaning, that when you vibrate in the Sadness frequency, you have the ability to magnify all of those particles into your reality.

ARCHANGEL METATRON SPEAKS:

"When you are working with the pineal gland, the thalamus and all that area of the brain, you are working with the magical scepter. The thalamus is the great pyramid because like any pyramid, it is the source of energy (light). You have a capstone that spins upon it which is the conductor sending the energy. However, even the capstone itself must receive the energy. When you look upon a pyramid, see it as a prism, a prism of light.

When you take a clear crystal quartz pyramid and you have light enter it, it then bends and reflects out like a stream. However, if you take a prism and it is hitting at a certain angle, not able to fully project out the entire spectrum of light, it may be stronger in the color Red. This is no different than if you are taking that crystal and holding it up for the Sun to reflect upon your wall. Sometimes it is so beautiful that you can see all the colors. This is no different than you are looking at it in the sky. Sometimes you can see all the colors in the sky and sometimes it is mainly strong in Pink hues.

When you look at those colors, let us now break them down into different dimensions and densities of existence, of physicality. If your mind is crystal clear of what is labeled as the Ego, the Ego Layers, meaning that it is fully collapsed to where you only have that crystal sheath of plasma (brain fluids), then the light is able to pass through smoothly to activate the pineal gland. Which is the capstone needed to project the information to the thalamus. It is from there that it can drip, drip, drip into your spine, which is your vertebrae housing your Angelic DNA. This is when you have those activations (DNA upgrades).

Now, when it comes to what you are able to perceive, not only as a conscious being, but in the physical world that is going to be that part of the spectrum that is emitted from your Magical Mind Scepter. Going back, reiterating, if you are only able to see a few colors that emit from that prism, that is blockage. That blockage is from emotions, stuck energy. Energy is meant to pass through. Along with that you have the consciousness field that is working with the mental programming, *meaning the Mental Body. Because, going back **Cracking the Chrysalis**, what we taught is the way you are able to work your Magical Mind Scepter, which projects the reality that you exist within, you created.*

You always have a blank canvas in every NOW moment. You are the master creator of what appears on that canvas. How do you do that. You go back to the basics. The e-MOTION~s. The Emotional Body, what is available there, that is your palette of "paint". The more emotionally available you are and open you are, then the more colors you have to choose from.

The paint brush is your Mental Body. The type of paint brush and once again, the availability that you have to use different types of brushes, that is determined by how mentally available and stable you are. That then becomes what you use to then project out through your Magical Mind Scepter, what is painted upon your reality.

The best example is the old saying of how you can look at life as a glass of water, half full or half empty. So, if you have an unbalanced Emotional and Mental mindset, you will see life as half empty. The spectrum we see most get stuck in is victimhood. If you are that negative person who likes to stay in the victimhood spectrum, let me blame the world and everyone else why I am what I am, when there is no one to blame because everything outside of you, you create. It is a mirrored reflection of what is in you.

If you have shadow aspects within you that need to be loved, healed, and balanced, because everything should be from a neutral viewpoint, then that is exactly what the world is going to show you. If you are constantly seeing the beauty in everyone and everything, then that is showing you simply who you are, because everything IS beautiful. It is all Divine.

This is what we ask you all to focus upon and go back to the basics."

Mind Prism Exercise

- On a piece of paper, draw 4 triangles.
- Write what is important to you for creating a clear mind crystal pyramid in each one.
- Draw a square.
- Write 4 actions you are committing to in order to maintain them on each of the 4 sides.

Mind Prism

Higher Mind Ascending
Zaneta Ra

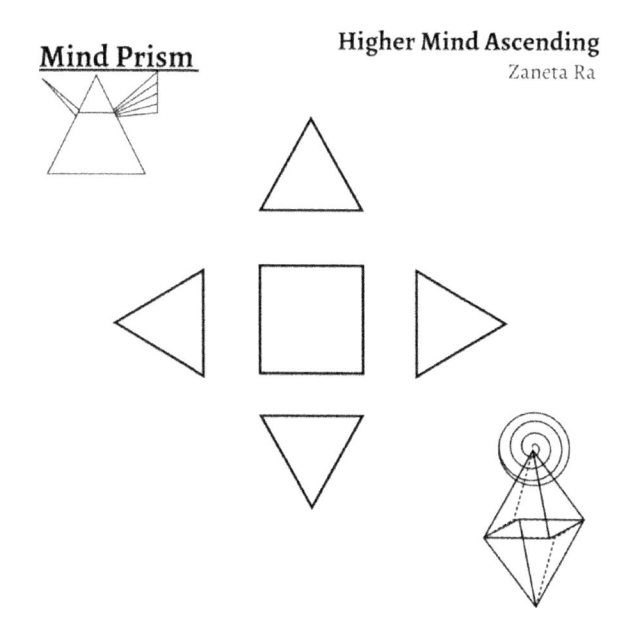

- Visualize connecting all the triangles to the square.
- Visualize this as the foundation for your mind crystal.
- Now point it down so the light can enter your body.
- See one pointed upward shining above your head in your pillar of light, this is your Higher Mind Crystal.
- Do weekly check-ins to visualize them and see your Higher Mind Crystal slowly descend.

- Do breathwork to feed the bright white light of your essence into your mind crystal.
- Each time you feel a shadow particle enter your mind, visualize cleaning your mind crystal.

> *Spin it at faster vibrational octaves until you see a white light flash.*
> *With your breath, expand this light until it bursts into fairy dust.*
> *See this dusting cleanse the shadow particle and transform it into gold.*

- At week 6, slowly inhale the light into your mind crystal.
- As you exhale *(mouth closed, keep the breath within your mind)*, project the light prism out of your 3rd Eye Chakra. Do this 3 times. You will feel a tingling sensation in your 3rd Eye. This is cleansing and expanding it.
- Do this exercise nightly before bed to allow your Higher Essence to flow through the body while it rests.

You will notice pin-pint diamond lights spark from time to time around you. This is your reality shifting into a higher density. Some will even see white whisp moving, these are your Spirit Guides. As you continue to this, you will notice your energy becoming more sensitive. It is simply the non-physical senses enhancing to accommodate your vibration.

For a more dedicated journey, please see our 6-month Energy Check-in Journal *(on Amazon)*.

Cracking the Chrysalis
Weekly Energy Check-in Journal

ATLANTIS

When you are fully anchored in the "now", you are anchored in an organic timeline. We teach of the inorganic timelines in *Angelic Pearls 144* and how many Lights were seeded in these planes to help stabilize the grid of the Universe. Those locusts started to multiply at such fast rates that we needed to send in more shield masters. However, for those masters to anchor, each of those incarnated warriors must help in collapsing The Lower Mind. The Lower Mind we speak of is the Astral, the collective thought-forms of the collective consciousness.

This collapsing is happening for those who are not able to discern the organic realities from the inorganic. Which will help them to finally exit the wheel of incarnation. This will also assist in the full bifurcation of the two Minds. The two Minds are also seen as the two Suns. Which got misconstrued to the two *sons* of God.

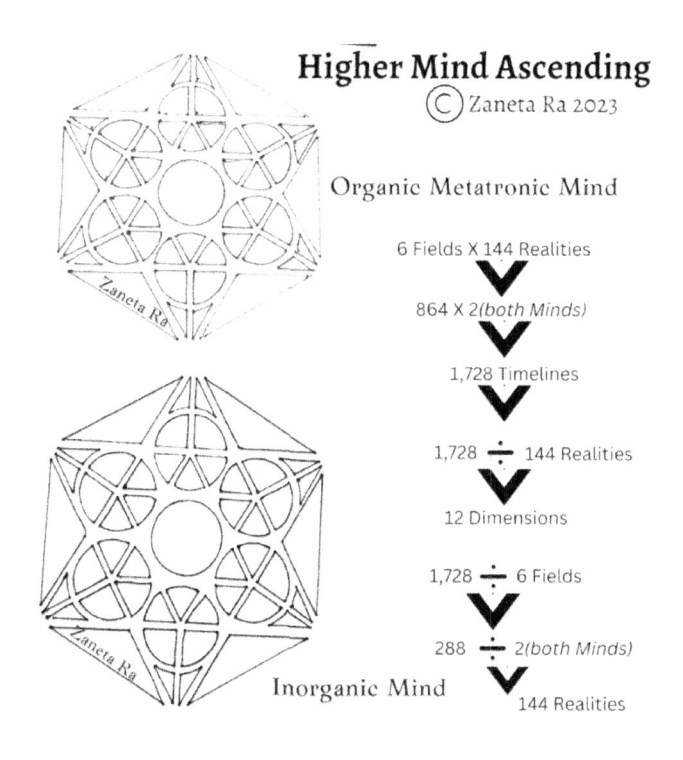

Higher Mind Ascending
© Zaneta Ra 2023

Organic Metatronic Mind

6 Fields X 144 Realities
▼
864 X 2 *(both Minds)*
▼
1,728 Timelines
▼
1,728 ÷ 144 Realities
▼
12 Dimensions

1,728 ÷ 6 Fields
▼
288 ÷ 2 *(both Minds)*
▼
144 Realities

Inorganic Mind

The fallen son is about the inorganic Sun created as the source of the inorganic timelines. These are the Atlantian consciousness fields. These fields exist in the linear Earth future, not the linear past of mankind.

You cannot simply erase or destroy a hijacked timeline because, by default, you automatically destroy that which is organic. In The Melchizedek Ur mandate an agreement was that this node in time and space, the very sector where your consciousness exists now, many will come to help save the fractalized souls that fell during the explosion of the holographic inorganic Earth.

This explosion is known as the fall of Atlantis. Atlantis does not occur on the organic timeline of Earth. This is a hijacked inorganic event that occurs on the infiltrated timeline. So many souls incarnated here hold deep wounds of Atlantis. Since all in creation happens in the now, that fragmented part of your soul is calling out to you of this node in time for help. On a parallel node of time, you exist directly across from the point in time Atlantis falls. The hijacked timeline will continue to play out because one should never intervene with nature.

When you balance your energetic bodies, work with your divine pearl-essence, it helps you to step out of these mind sets and into your diamond pillar of Christos light. This then generates your very own grid of diamonds that automatically transmute any inorganic energy waves that come into your field. This is the meaning of the eye of storm. A storm of energy can be whirling around you however it cannot harm you. Your very own Christos light is your guardian angel.

~Angelic Pearls 144

The meaning of the "fallen son" references a Sun which is of a lower vibrational spectrum. Held within every Sun is a Seed Crystal. This is the lifeforce energy of that Sun. It is from this crystal that arms of energy extend out to feed all life forms held within its toroidal field. For your local Sun this is known as a Solar System.

The way this inorganic crystal was created was through absorbing Christos energy from other Seed Crystals. In every Angelic being there is a Light Seed which is given by God Source at the moment of Creation. It is from this seed that light can emit out to all fractals that descend from it. For example, your Seed Crystal is with your Pearl-essence/Monad/Oversoul. It feeds light through your multi-dimensional DNA strands into all fractals/aspects of itself. Around these strands is a plasma diamond sheath.

Some of these sheaths were tampered with, creating a vortex within them. This vortex allowed energy to flow from it, like a stream from a river. The new stream of light was fed into a new source, in this case was the inorganic Sun. It is this Sun that we call the Atlantian consciousness. From this many technological timelines were created.

This plasma cord connects to your 9th Chakra and is the connection for your consciousness.

Higher Mind Ascending
Zaneta Ra

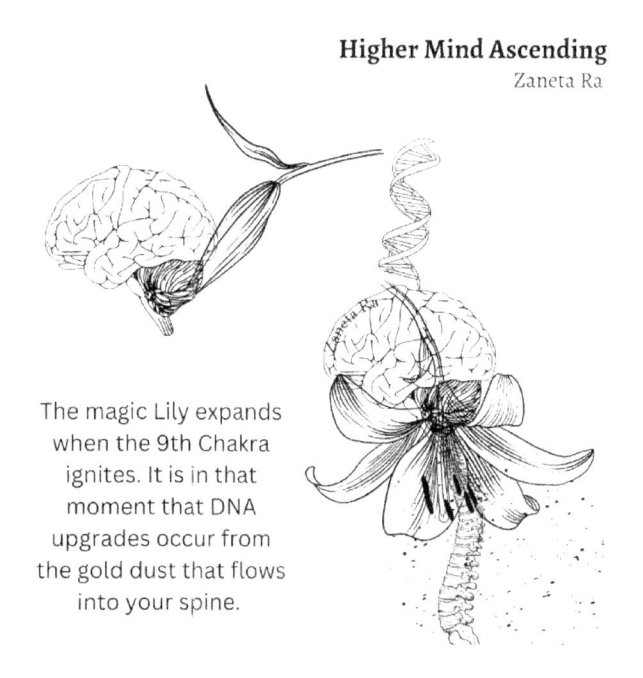

The magic Lily expands when the 9th Chakra ignites. It is in that moment that DNA upgrades occur from the gold dust that flows into your spine.

The gold dust is your Christos energy pollen. It is what houses creator software *(they do not mean literally but using as a vibrational likeness)*. Without this software one is unable to access Christ Codes. These are codes that can be used to create blueprints/grids/matrices for materialized worlds.

Atlan Mind

The Atlantis field can be seen as an infinity mirror of labyrinths. These are fed from a portal that connects to the organic grids.

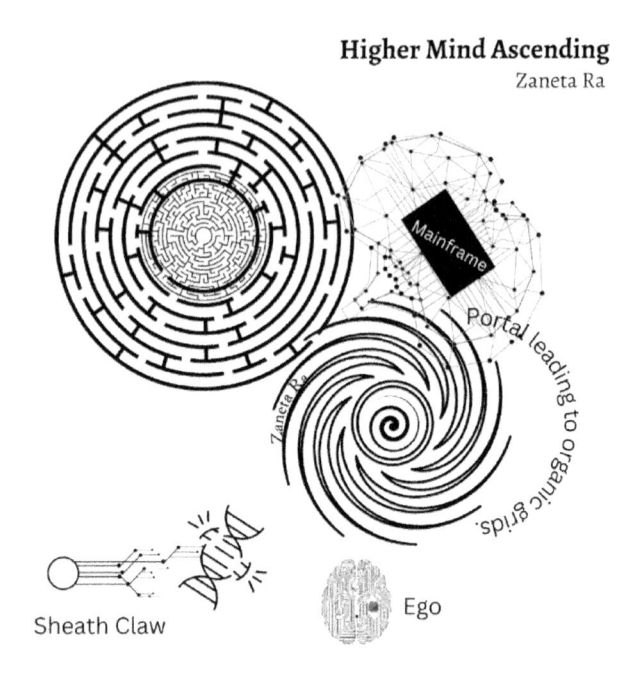

Higher Mind Ascending
Zaneta Ra

Sheath Claw

Ego

The sheath claw seen in the image is what connects into your multi-dimensional DNA to harness the Christos energy. It also places the Ego Mind insert. The Ego Mind as we have disclosed in the Pearl Code Teachings, is inorganic. This is an unseen energy that was part of an anchoring from the inorganic Atlantis Planes.

ARCHANGEL METATRON SPEAKS:

"When it comes to that which is known as "Atlantis", this is deeper than the mortal mind can comprehend. "Atlantis" is not a land, or a physical place made of Earthly elements. Instead, it is a consciousness field that holds a technological vibrational core. Source can be seen as THE MIND and all of existence is merely a thought-form. The original thought and the flow of that vibration is a timeline. There are those who oversee these thoughts/timelines to make sure they stay in alignment with the Divine Will. Divine Will simply is the spoken word of Source God.

However, if energy within a thought-form wants to merge from the organic flow, then it causes what is known as an "Inorganic" timeline to form. This newly formed path has created a new entry point (portal/gateway) where the energy that flows down the organic path can veer off. This is like a river who has newly formed streams running from it.

Since inorganic energy and technology was created in slightly Higher Worlds, it is not stabilized. For it to become stabilized it needs to have an anchor point in the densest fields. When this new energy is anchored at the dense fields of existence it allows more force to flow into the Higher Worlds. Atlantis is an inorganic

Time-Space Reality that terminated within itself due to the unestablished energetic patterns. For it to become more stabilized and hold more force it needs more chaotic energy. This energy is created when Souls become fractalized, which starts with seeded chaotic thoughts.

The mission occurring now is to place a dam door where the stream connects to the river. As you see, this means traveling backwards in time to where it was created. This is how we can best explain the creation of Atlantis occurring in the linear future, because where you all reside is at this connection point. You can see this divide in your existence today, the bifurcation stage.

When you raise your consciousness, it helps to raise the DNA lineage you incarnated into both forwards and backwards in time, we call this para-genetics. What this is doing is helping to heal any damaged DNA that is in those lines. Since the combined DNA of the collective is what the Earth Grid feeds from, this directly affects its timelines. Meaning, when the DNA is upgraded in vibration, so too are the timelines.

The reason elect Souls came to incarnate at this now time node is to help anchor their higher DNA energy. In order to assist with upgrading the DNA of the collective, the Solar Ones came. This is the bloodline of the organic Sun. When they came into this system, they passed through a Solar Gateway that created a Solar Body able to hold these Solar Codes.

By bringing their Light Seed and these codes into a human form, it helped to upgrade DNA held within the body. They also were able to filter through the body and their Light Body these Solar Codes. These codes fed into the surface Earth Grid lines and into her Inner Seed Crystal for upgrades. This helps to fully anchor her Crystal to the organic grid system." (***Zaneta Ra:*** *For the complete teaching on the Solar Tribes please read **Angelic Pearls 144**)*

When you experience a Higher Mind Awakening, it is collapsing the Ego Mind. This causes the vibrational field of your mind to expand and raise. When you interact with another living being *(man, animal, nature etc.)* it helps to raise their awareness as well. In some cases, your Light Bodies exchange codes. A higher octave Light Body will communicate codes to the other that will seed into their subconsciousness. When they reach the vibrational frequency *(keycode)* to access that code, then it will ignite like popcorn into their consciousness.

This can also work on the negative spectrum. If you are interacting with someone who has those locusts swarming around them, they can come to your field and try to lower your vibrations through thoughts. This again, can only occur if your Emotional Body holds any particles with a like vibration of those negative thought forms. An example of this is when you are feeling great, but then get a phone call from someone who unloads their emotional baggage onto you. When you hang up the phone you feel a sudden drop in your energy.

If you feel sudden fatigue, then it is because you took into your light field those locusts and transmuted them. This is something to be mindful of because the other person is subconsciously emotional dumping. If this is done too often it can cause your Light Body to lower in vibration. This is why Psychic Mediums and Healers have it hard, they are selflessly helping to transmute particles in other's Emotional Bodies, both alive and departed.

Having conscious mindfulness is going to be your biggest support during this process. Take time for stillness, reflection, and gratitude for yourself.

MIND CRYSTALS

Every creation in existence has mind crystals. The Universal Mind has an extension of 144 of them, known as the 144 Universal Suns *(See **Angelic Pearls 144**).* Since this mind is of such a high vibration, it is invisible in your current plane. Your local Sun is fed indirectly from this mind. Earth is fed by the local Sun through a diamond cord that is anchored in her core.

In her core is a plasma diamond Sun known as her heart crystal. The light from her heart crystal emits out and as it densifies, it creates physical crystals. These crystals are the materialized form of planetary neurotransmitters. These are the messengers of the mind that carry light transmissions. Each crystal is designed to carry specific vibrations, which are coded light transmissions.

Learning how each spectrum of Creation carries light particles, imagine them densified into crystals. This can help you to understand why there are unlimited crystals. When we speak of crystals, we are also speaking of all metals, rocks, and seashells. Seashells are extremely high in vibration. Many of you coded them long ago with information for this time node.

Andara Crystals

Andara crystals are glasslike high vibrational crystals that became known in the 1990s. They emerged because the collective had reached a vibrational frequency to receive them. Each time the consciousness grid is raised, it has entered a new density. This allows beings such as Andara crystals to coexist in your reality.

These are connected directly to the Suns of Venus, Pleiades, Andromeda, and Sirius. Let us state that there are many types of Andara crystals and only 1 species has emerged thus far on your planet. A new one will emerge in the next vibrational grid octave *(**Zaneta Ra:** Between now-2025. Autumn 2023-Autumn 2024 many new crystals will emerge).*

Many feel a connection to the Lemurian consciousness because of their frequency. As you learn in ***Love Letters from Lemuria***, Lemuria is not one place, it is a consciousness expression that exists in multiple dimensions. It also is not expressed in this Universe but stems from the Morana Universe.

When an attempt to infiltrate that Universe occurred, these light transmissions were brought here by the Solar Tribes and Elect Souls directly from Venus. They were time locked and coded to emerge with select keys. Remember, the keys to access Light Codes are a specific vibrational frequency. These can be likened to binary codes for a computer.

One person can hold a crystal and access limited information, while another can hold it and access unlimited information. This is because of the key code access one has access to, which again, is determined by their vibration.

Most of the ones found today are coded to activate DNA for the Higher Mind Awakening stage to become engaged. Some will even notice head pain after holding these crystals. It is due to the information being streamed through the Myelin Axons found in your brain. These are streaming light into your Peripheral and Central Nervous Systems. This then causes sensations in the spine due to the upgrades occurring for your DNA.

Some have keys to access information directly from the Universal Sun located in Morana from these crystals. These are going to be those that are completely clear. You can tell this by your first interaction with them. When you connect with them, they will show you the blue diamond Sun. It is from there you can access the codes.

This is done because all crystals are connected like a web multi-dimensionally. They are DNA for all Mind Crystals. Each one connected to their own spectrum. All quartz is connected to their own webbing. All emeralds to their own etc.

Atlantis Crystals

Atlantis crystals are clear Andara crystals that are currently found in the caves of Arkansas, USA. They have only found select ones however, an influx is about to occur. The Christos energy harnessed and used to create the Atlantis timelines can be found in those crystals. The energy we speak of are only of the streams selected by God Source be returned. What occurred is when those timelines failed, the energy from the Atlan mind crystals were rescued and placed in those crystals *(Arkansas)*.

It is because of this connection that many feel an essence that belongs to a Soul in them, known as a Soul fragment. This is because it is. It was dedicated to this time node and grid system so it can be returned to that Soul. This happens in three ways:

1. That Soul is incarnated, and the crystal is brought into their field. Through their Light Body, the energy is retrieved, healed, recycled.

2. A Grid Worker is able to access the energy of the crystal caves to retract the Soul essence and return to Source through one of the God Portals.
3. Crystals are brought into the field of the incarnated 144,144 for them to either send home to God Source or give to the Soul incarnated.

What most are doing with Atlantis crystals is helping to balance the timelines. This is mostly not done consciously. Remember those beautiful diamond sparkles around you? It is those sparkles that are re-coding those crystals. This in turn is streaming energy to those timelines. What it is also doing is helping to place caps where the stream connects to the river. What we mean here, is closing inorganically designed portal systems.

Crystal Portals

Crystal portals are created when two beings are interacting. This can mean you speaking with another incarnate or an interdimensional being. The energy from the mind crystals start to extend and lace together for an exchange of information.

This is how your Guides/Spirit Team can send you images via Clairvoyance/Telepathy.

In order for this process to run smoothly, both mind crystals must be clear. If it is not clear, then the message will be staticky. Think back to what Metatron taught of the light spectrum emitting from a clear crystal pyramid.

When it comes to you interacting with another human, if one is unbalanced then it can also cause static or friction to occur in the energy fields. This will trigger sudden irritation and annoyance. It is at that moment we suggest a step back to reflect on yourself *(if you are the one who was triggered)*. It also means that the one who felt stronger static has a blockage in their energy field. This is going to be either in their Emotional or Mental Body. This is why you have those interactions in the first place. People and events are ignited to help bring awareness into your field. It is simply up to you to notice it.

These crystal portals are also active when you connect with crystals, animals, trees, elements etc. Everything around you are living conscious beings. It is the power of the mind that can communicate with them. The elements are easy to speak to because they are what your form is made from. When you are in water, take time to connect your heart and mind to it. Feel yourself become it and it become you. Allow this connection to play like a movie reel in your mind. Do not think, just be and allow the water to speak to you.

Do this with a tree. Place one hand on its trunk and another on your heart. Close your eyes and unite with it. Send it love and feel it vibrate love to you in return. It is rarely that you will hear words or a voice. It is simply through the vibrations we emit to your mind crystals that send those signals of information to you. Just remember that the more balanced your energy field is, the clearer your channels will be.

THE NIGHT

The word night stems from the Greek goddess Nyx and the Egyptian goddess Neith. It is even connected to the ancient name of the Nile River An-Nil. All of which translates to *nothingness*. Night simply is a realm of darkness, of the void. You came to the opposite spectrum of the macro void, the womb of NO-THING, to be reborn. In order to truly know *Who I am*, to see all your light, you must travel to the depths of the darkness.

The process of Ascension is simple. Unconsciously humans want to make it hard because that is how life is programmed to be. It is programmed as an illusion of enslavement. At this point in your journey, it is time to dissolve those chains of illusions. It is time for you to fly from the mental cage you have encased yourself within.

"It is not until you traverse the body of flesh, that you will have conquered the dark night of the Soul. For the night is the Underworld, a place you come to remember your light."

~Zaneta Ra

When you rise above the flesh and see who you are, you will dissolve any feelings of unworthiness and emptiness. For you are ALL and you are connected to ALL. The pupil of the eye only expands in the darkness. It needs that darkness to expand and so do you. The light needs shadows to reflect who it is. The shadows need light to see who it is.

All of existence is a balancing act. All of existence dances and sways with each other. It is only when you resist moving that contraction pains intensify.

Universal Truth simply is and that is existence itself. When the mind wants to ask questions, whom is this feeding? What will this accomplish? Ask yourself these questions when your mind starts to ponder. Is this feeding the mind of the mortal or of the Spirit.

The Spirit knows ALL because it is ALL. A Light Master simply allows information to flow into them, instead of constantly seeking answers for the mind. They do not get distracted or lost searching in the weeds. They simply glide through the valley and allow the rays of the Sun to guide them.

Dawn Symptoms

Symptoms known as the *Dawn* are what occur at the cusp of your Higher Mind Awakening and anchoring. We call it *Dawn Symptoms* because this is a time when the light of your Sun *(Solar Self)* starts to appear. As you traverse the Night these symptoms will arise during this stage. The following information is for those who started this as of June 2023, which is the first wave of the Higher Mind Awakening. There will be many other waves that follow, and these Dawn Symptoms will occur for each wave group.

This process occurs in three steps with each one typically lasting 30-42 days. The first wave group has already anchored in the 5D-7D timeline wave fields. It is this stage of your Ascension that will help to anchor all your Energy Bodies onto those time waves. The last ones to anchor are your Mental and Physical Bodies.

The Emotional and Mental Bodies must become mastered because in those time waves manifestation occurs instantly. Before you can finish a thought, it is done. If your emotional and mental states are unbalanced, then it will cause those time waves to crash into each other. This will cause the energy of those Higher Planes to become unbalanced.

Step I

The energies of the upcoming summer season will be that of intense heat. This heat is from the Light Codes that will enter your physical field. From January to April 2023, those codes anchored from your Higher Pearl-essence unto your Light

Body. Those who felt vertigo and extreme fatigue during that time are due to this anchoring. These codes will be felt most intensely in the Crown, 9th, and Solar Plexus Energy Centers *(Chakras)*.

This integration will be occurring until the end of August. The first stage will be in the Crown. This is causing many of you to have an overactive mind due to the Ego death stage occurring. You will find moments where the mind feels like it is about to explode from overloads. In those moments take time for stillness and inwardness. Take walks in nature, swim, be active, and creative. This will help these energies to flow into you in a smoother nature.

Symptoms of the Crown Chakra Integration:

- Intense Migraines
- Overactive Mind
- Obsession with a Spiritual Ascension Topic *(mainly on shadow ones)*
- Crown tingles
- Broken Record replay of past traumatic events *(they are trying to collapse)*

- Third Eye throbs *(due to 5D activations)*
- Ear and Nose sensitivity *(mostly the left ear)*
- Some may have a change in taste/food cravings *(especially potatoes and fruit)*
- Extreme thirst
- Insomnia/new sleep patterns
- Several Déjà vu moments *(timeline jumping)*
- Visions of Archangel Metatron and/or Seraphina in dreams/visions/meditations

The key to helping this flow is to not try to dissect the energy but to allow it to flow. Remember, all of existence is energy and meant to simply FLOW through you. Light a candle and look at it for 33 minutes to help quiet the mind chatter. See yourself in that light, allow it to reflect your own light.

Step II

The next stage is the 9th, Chakra. As more are becoming plugged into their Higher Pearl-essence they will feel this tingling of energy at the base of their skull. This is because light coming directly from your wholeness, your OverSoul/Monad/Pearl-essence is dripping into your spine. It allows those higher vibrational multi-dimensional DNA codes to anchor into your vertebrae. They will then move to grow at your thymus and disperse into your bloodstream-organs etc.

Symptoms of the 9th Chakra/God Portal Integration:

- New wisdom emerging in your field
- New higher timeline memories
- Desire for alone time
- Increase desire for meditation
- Spine tingles
- Extreme temperatures in the spine such as coolness/hotness
- Desire to dance like a serpent *(helps to move the energy for better anchoring)*
- Orgasmic feelings within
- Sore neck and shoulder pain

- Cracking in the 9th Chakra area when moving the neck
- Some will have soreness between shoulder blades *(due to DNA expanding in the Heart Crystal area)*

Step III

The next stage will be in the Solar Plexus area. As taught in the Pearl Code books; there is a diamond light cord located at the belly button that plugs into the Divine Cosmic Ocean. This is where the lifeforce energy is fed to all of creation. All the core wounds *(especially in women)* are held in this area. Most Empaths and Psychic Mediums carry more body fat around the stomach as an unconscious protection of their lifeforce energy. Some hold body fat here due to suppressed childhood emotions.

As your Energic Bodies *(including the physical body)* are shifting from being anchored in the 3rd Density Realities to the 5th Density realities, you are collapsing those lower 3 Chakras. This is happening with the Stage II Lightworkers mostly. What is occurring is all of the energy that no longer serves you is being pulled to this Energy

Center. It is ready to be released through the diamond light cord at your belly button.

Symptoms of the Solar Plexus Integration:

- Unable to push the breath past the stomach
- Leg tingles
- Leg electric shocks at night
- Tingles in the soles of your feet at night
- Hip pain
- Sciatica pain
- Diarrhea
- Frequent upset stomach
- Sensitive stomach
- Desire to fast some days or to only juice *(this is because soon you will need to eat as much food and instead live off light mana)*
- Desire for more breath work and body movement *(especially in the legs)*
- Heart palpitations *(especially at night or when the body first wakes up)*

As this integration completes, some will start to see geometric patterns around objects. This is how the ancient buildings found around the world were able to be built so perfectly. The vision to see geometric light patterns of all material forms is part of the higher timeline abilities.

Most of the physical symptoms will occur at night when the physical body is more at rest. You will also notice an increase in electric shocks happening at night. To gain a better understanding of the physical transformation your body is going through please read **The Ascension Symptoms Manual**. We created that manual for you all to have better clarity.

We ask that you all take it easy on your body and your mind. Flow as ONE with the river of existence. The energy river of your wholeness that flows through you. Know that you are not alone in this, you are never alone and we, the Angels walk beside you every step of THE WAY.

"I am the cosmic water lily that rose shining from Nun's black primordial waters, and my mother is Nut, the night sky. O you who made me, I have arrived, I am the great ruler of yesterday, the power of command is in my hand."

~The Book of the Dead

MIND CODE MEDITATIONS

This section is designed with Light Codes for you to meditate upon. These are coded with a vibrational elixir to help heighten your mind crystals. You can have fun with this by closing your eyes and asking your Spirit to guide you to the one to start with. There are a few ways to work with them. Use what feels best in your heart. Take a week's break if it causes any pain. Do not overwork yourself, allow your body time to rest and upgrade.

OPTION A

1-Ask your Spirit team to show you what needs to be healed.

2-Meditate while looking at it for 10 minutes.

3-Allow emotions to surface during that time. No thinking, just FEEL them with the body.

4-When you are done, write down on a piece of paper what you felt.

5-Close your eyes and ask your Spirit team to show you why you feel this way.

6-Speak out loud what you see to allow the images to play.

7-Ask your Spirit team to help you release what no longer serves you. Ask that only what is for your highest good and your Ascension journey remain.

8-After the ceremony, place your hand on you heart and say:

"I thank you.

I thank you.

I thank you.

I love you.

I love me.

I love we.

*I am ALL and ALL is we for ALL
eternity."*

OPTION B

1-Ask your Spirit team to activate your Angelic DNA.
2-Look at an image for 10 seconds.
3-Close your eyes and take a deep slow breath into your mind.
4-See the breath enter a crystal pyramid.
5-Hold the breath there while counting to 3.
6-Slowly exhale *(with the mouth closed)* out of your third eye.
7-Do this again but this time visualize bright white light entering the pyramid and observe what color(s) exit your third eye.
8-Repeat #7 again.
9-Take a slow deep breath into your heart.
10-Hold it and count to 3.
11-Slowly exhale *(with the mouth closed)* out of your shoulder blades.
12-Repeat steps 9-11 again, this time when you inhale: lend your shoulders back. When you exhale: lend your shoulders forward.
13-Repeat #12, but with a larger inhale.

14-Lift your arms up to the sky and slowly bring them back down, hands up to create a door and place in front of your heart.
15-Say to yourself:

> *"I am complete.*
>
> *I am whole.*
>
> *I am LOVE."*

Higher Mind Awakening
Zaneta Ra

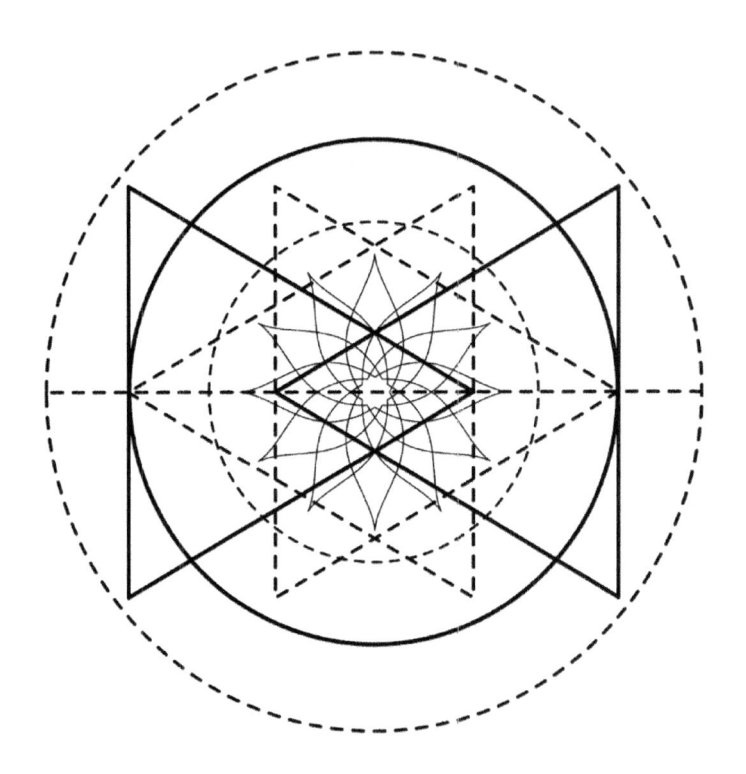

Higher Mind Awakening
Zaneta Ra

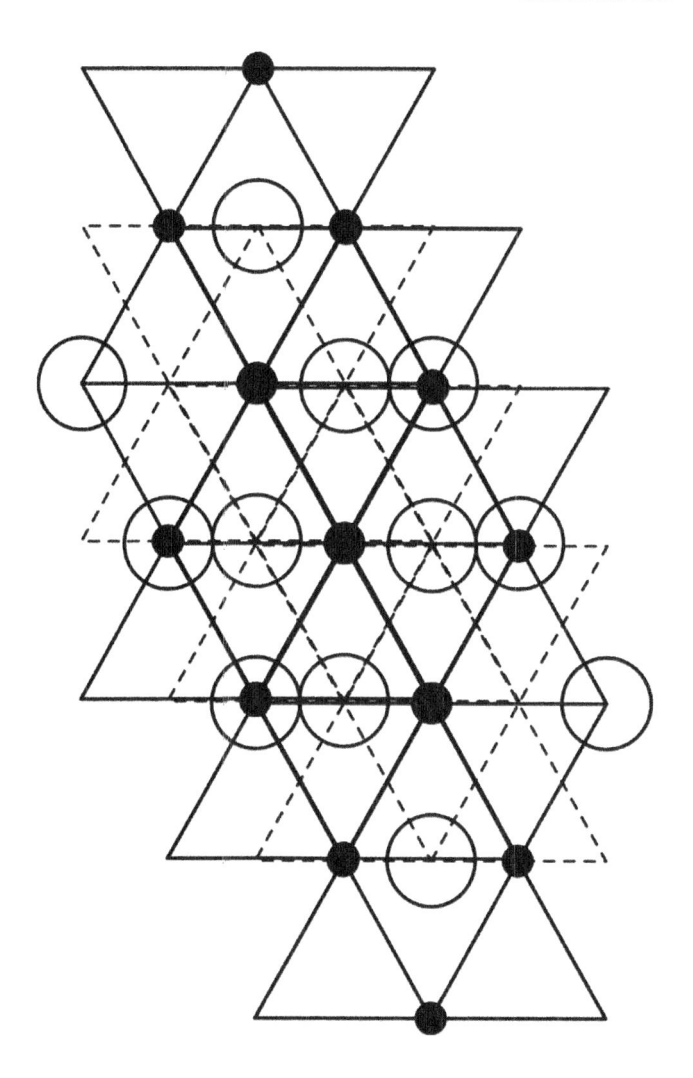

Higher Mind Awakening
Zaneta Ra

Higher Mind Awakening
Zaneta Ra

Higher Mind Awakening
Zaneta Ra

Higher Mind Awakening
Zaneta Ra

Higher Mind Awakening
Zaneta Ra

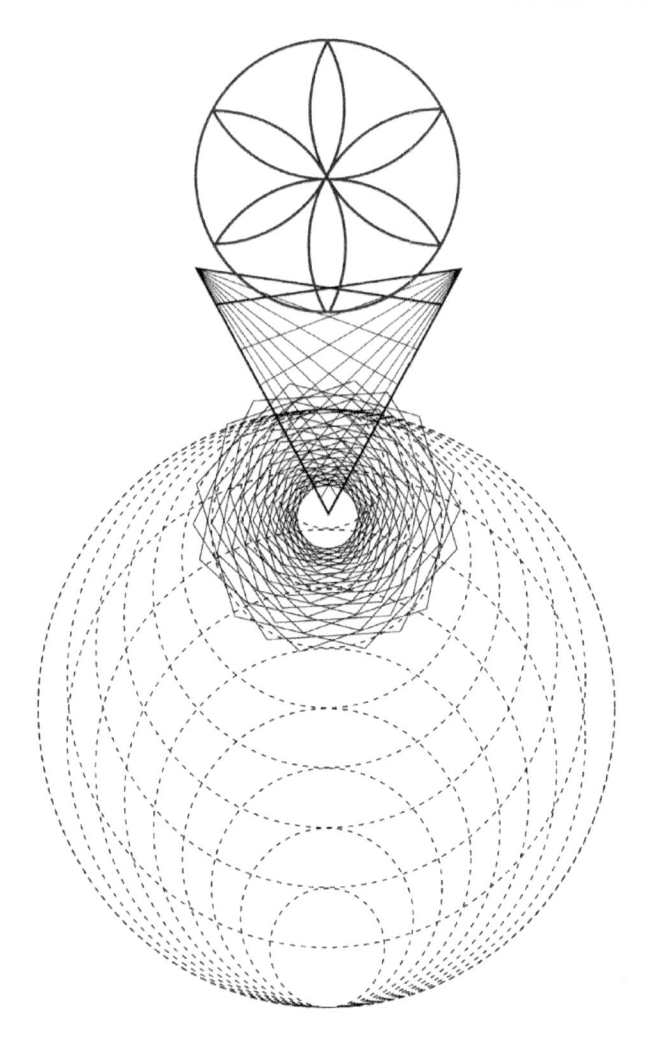

Higher Mind Awakening
Zaneta Ra

Higher Mind Awakening
Zaneta Ra

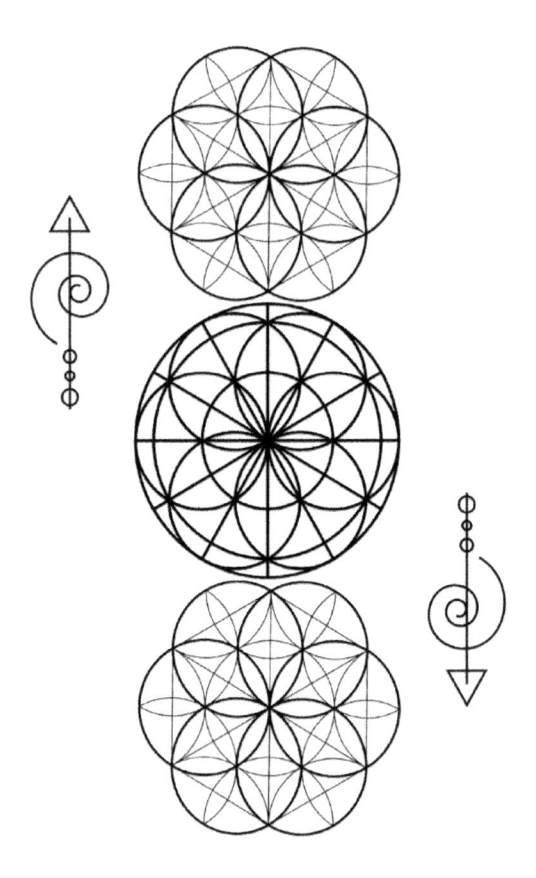

Higher Mind Awakening
Zaneta Ra

Higher Mind Awakening
Zaneta Ra

Higher Mind Awakening
Zaneta Ra

Excerpt from Instill the Grain: Oracles, Gods and Goddesses

The goddess Nike is associated with holding a rowan wreath and a reed. The reed is associated with the Scorpio segment upon the Zodi wheel. This signifies the serpent fire, which is your Soul. The reed is seen in ancient Celtic Druid teachings as the symbol of the Soul. It is taught that Scylla (sea serpent), Zelus (fiery), Via/Bia (force), and Kratos (power) are siblings of Nike, in reality these are simply aspects. These all signify a personality held within your own serpent fire. The other siblings spoken of are Fontes (fountains) and Lacus (Lakes) which merely signify your Soul stream where you drink your own serpent fire.

As seen in the Zodi wheel, the rowan tree is associated with the Capricorn segment. This is connected to the crowning one receives when their ascension is engaged. The word cap is found in Capricorn for this reason. The color of wild corn is seen as purple, which signifies the Christos energy. Corn is also associated with the harvesting of the Soul.

The rowan tree is called Sorbus in Latin; it is from sor that you get the meaning red. This is where red associated with the holiday Christmas comes from. It is truly the name Nik this archetype essence holds. From Nik you find the name Nicolas, who is associated with the same holiday. The Christmas tree signifies the lighting up of your Kundalini or all Chakras needed before you can become crowned by the Christos.

It is not that a physical man was "crucified" on a rowan tree like spoken of in the more recent years, it simply signifies your own Christos light bound within the in-between. What we mean by this is that field of energy where the Seen and Unseen Worlds do not exist. This is outside of time yet also inside of time. It is within existence yet outside of existence. We speak in riddles for this is a coded transmission meant for you to decipher not with the mortal mind. The legends spoken of do not literally mean any of that which is used by the tongue to express. It is only from that which is unheard and from that which is unseen can you find the answers that you seek beautiful sparks of THE LIGHT.

The term victory is associated with this god archetype. Yet, what does that mean to you? Victory in the English tongue expresses an achievement of MASTERY. When you subtract the energy fields that the mortal resides in, you will discover that this does not mean an achievement of war. Victory means to become a victor of your own internal battle. It means to overcome that of the seen realms, to become a master and fly upon the golden sandals into the Gateway of the Sun.

Excerpt from The Ascension Symptoms Manual

The Pituitary Gland is located at the base of the brain near the hypothalamus. Its main function is to regulate bodily functions through the 9 hormones it produces. This is a master gland that monitors and regulates the bodily functions of key players like the kidneys, uterus, adrenal glands, and the thyroid gland. If this gland is not producing certain hormones properly it can cause issues such as blood pressure, growth issues, and the inability to reproduce.

Tibetan Spiritualism teaches of a "white drop" that is always located at the Crown Chakra and descends towards the heart center once the four physical elements have dissolved. This can be seen as the white light that drips into the Pineal to then drip into the Pituitary. The Pituitary then descends it through your body to be anchored at your Thymus. This is where the crystalline petals of our Higher Heart expand to anchor the Christ Seed.

It is during this stage some feel as if they are dying. Well, because you are, as in the old self and the Ego Mind. Typically, before this stage occurs your taste buds change, and that physical taste sense shuts down. This can be accompanied by coughing up mucus because of new White Blood Cell production. Hence the "white drop" (For more learning see the Buddhist Wheel of Life). As plasma light densifies it can shift into the form, we call White Blood Cells.

Excerpt from Love Letters from Lemuria

Da'Kini Ash'tara: The City of Seraphim can be accessed by your Inner Planes. We are interconnected with the inner cities of the sphere you call Venus as well as the local Sun. We are the main Sun city and known as the blue fire. It is here the legends of dragons were birthed because the sacred breath, the Ra of the Holy Mother Dragon, formed it. The sacred legends of King Arthur are connected here. The legends of Avalon are connected here. The legends of Unicorns, Fae, Merlins, Elves, Druids, Valkyries, Gods, and Goddesses are connected here. Many Ascended Masters and Angels teach here as well as some of you in your dream state.

The blue fire city calls to you because you come here often and most of you are anchored here, not to the surface plane. You are anchored to the core of the magical realms and leave golden dust footprints everywhere you go. Let us take a walk through the doorways of your memory as I help you re-remember the magical Inner Planes.

All the Kingdoms of Ur have their own expression of Divine's Will that we help to make sure is conducted. We receive these Light Codes mainly as plasma orbs that house the Divine Blueprints. We have a Diamond River that we, the magical Da'Kini, retrieve them from. We are a mix of Fairies, Elves, and those called the Shining Ones.

This river is part of what is known in legends as the Milky River. Here, in a higher density, the river appears as diamond light with a slight milkiness to it. It flows from the local Sun and through all the planetary bodies. This truly is the diamond light string of the Solar System pearl necklace. As it flows through our city, the orbs glow that are of a vibrational match for this planetary sphere. We then retrieve them, read them, separate them, and disperse them.

BOOKS BY ZANETA RA

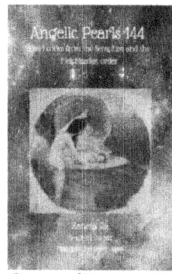

Advance Level Learning

Angelic Pearls 144
Pearl codes from the Seraphim and the Melchizedek order
ISBN: 9798428688535

Rising Merits
The 42 Pearl Temples of Ancient Egypt
ISBN: 979 8804058464

Intermediate Level Learning

The Pearl Light Codes
44 Light Activations from the Seraphim
ISBN: 9798438477693

Cracking the Chrysalis
Shattering the Steps of Ascension
ISBN: 9798840365298

Introductory Level

The Ascension Symptoms Manual

ISBN:979-8356257346

The **Ascension Symptoms Manual** breaks down:

- Physical Symptoms
- Emotional Symptoms
- Mental Symptoms
- Psyche Symptoms
- Light Code Symptoms
- Psychic Abilities
- Plasma Diamond Light Body
- Substances Negatively Enhancing Ascension Symptoms and much more.

All books available on Amazon in Paperback, eBook, and Hardcover

ISBN: 9798366416047

On Amazon in Paperback, Hardcover, and eBook

- 144 Lemurian Light Codes
- Meri-Ra-Ka Healing

With messages from Light Masters from Lemuria, Venus, the Sun, Inner Earth, the Morana Universe and more.

ISBN: 9798376554913

On Amazon in Paperback, Hardcover, and eBook

Instill the Grain breaks down:
- Who the gods are
- Why Oracles were created
- The origins of the Zodiac
- The original Temple teachings
- What are Mortal and Immortal Souls
- What is The Garden
- Over 80 God Aspects
- Transmissions from Zeus, Thor, and Artemis
- What does the crescent and the Sun Door mean, and much more.

Light Warrior Journals

Angelic Pearls
Journal

Cracking the Chrysalis
Weekly Energy Check-in
Journal

6 Month Energy Tracker Journal designed to help you manage your energy field.

ILLUSTRATIONS

Hercules and Lernaean
https://upload.wikimedia.org/wikipedia/commons/1/1b/Singer_Sargent%2C_John_-_Hercules_-_1921.jpg
John Singer Sargent, Public domain, via Wikimedia Commons

Bee Goddess
https://upload.wikimedia.org/wikipedia/commons/a/a1/Plaque_bee-goddess_BM_GR1860.4-123.4.jpg
British Museum, Public domain, via Wikimedia Commons

Hercules Killing the Stymphalian Birds
https://upload.wikimedia.org/wikipedia/commons/3/36/1500_Duerer_Herkules_im_Kampf_gegen_die_stymphalischen_Voegel_anagoria.JPG
Albrecht Dürer, Public domain, via Wikimedia Commons

Apis bull

https://upload.wikimedia.org/wikipedia/commons/e/e4/Api_or_Hapi_%28Apis%2C_Taureau_Consacr%C3%A9_a_la_Lune%29%2C_N372.2.jpg
Léon-Jean-Joseph Dubois, Public domain, via Wikimedia Commons

Isis Knot, Tyet
https://upload.wikimedia.org/wikipedia/commons/0/07/Tit_%28Isis_knot%29_amulet_MET_DP109370.jpg
Metropolitan Museum of Art, CC0, via Wikimedia Commons

St. Mark's Basilica, Venice Floor mosaic by Paolo Uccello, Small stellated dodecahedron
https://upload.wikimedia.org/wikipedia/commons/9/95/Marble_floor_mosaic_Basilica_of_St_Mark_Vencice.jpg
Paolo Uccello, Public domain, via Wikimedia Commons

Printed in Great Britain
by Amazon